Come and See

There's No More

Powerful Time Than

Now

to Discover How

to Create Enduring,

Lasting Success

by Actually

"Acting Upon Your Life"

Rather than

Having it

"Act Upon You"

Permanently!

Copyright © 2003 Rene L. Messier. Printed and bound in Canada. All rights reserved. No part of this book may be reproduced or transmitted in any form or by any means, electronic or mechanical, including photocopying, recording, or by an information storage or retrieval system – except by a reviewer who may quote brief passages in a review to be printed in a magazine or newspaper – without permission in writing from the publisher. For information, contact Sage Academy Books, #9101 - 10900 NE 8th Street 9th Flr. Bellevue, Washington, USA 98004 - 4448 or in Canada 15020 75 Avenue Surrey, B.C. Canada V3S 6S3 or email @ info@sageacademy.com

Library of Congress Control Number: 2003095820

ISBN 0-9742494-0-8

The terms *FaithSkills*, *FaithSkills* Personal Operating System, *FaithSkills* Success Series, Success Builders and The Affiliated Sage are Trade Marked Products ™ of Sage Support Services Inc. Trade Marks pending.

Published by: Sage Academy Books

Printed in the United States

Editor – Patricia (Trish) Sutton
Cover Designer – Kami Morris of *Saliant Graphic and Design*
Book & Page Designer – Kami Morris of *Saliant Graphic and Design*
Proof Readers – Carmen Friesen, Violy Mecham, Kim Aippersbach
Consumer Research – The Sage Research Institute

Here's what people are saying about this powerful material!

"You're onto something huge. This is a quantum leap and the key to success. Every person, every businessperson, every business leader needs this. It's Incredible!"

Del Ball – Independent Business Consultant

"Thanks for writing such an inspiring and helpful book. It is the first thing that has come close to explaining faith in a language and format I can understand."

Cathy Price - Port Allen, Human Resources Officer

"Just as how to achieve financial freedom is not taught in our formal schooling neither is how to achieve freedom from our own negative thoughts and behavior - Rene Messier has identified a pattern of success and the skill sets needed to reach our higher purpose in life. If you can master the skills in this book you can master life."

M.J. Bester P.Eng, P.M.P. - Mediator & Project Manager

"Applying the principles of *FaithSkills* will most definitely improve anyone's quality of life."

Joe Singh, President – Alliance Auto Parts

"*FaithSkills* is a must read for anyone struggling with their self identity...not only does it comfort the reader through it's short introductory stories that we are all traveling the same journeys....it also educates the reader how to make those journeys successful ones."

Niya Harper - Professional Homemaker & Pharmacy Technician.

"I have been so motivated by your book – *FaithSkills*. It has made me realize that there is so much un-tapped human potential in me and everyone else."

Jo Wiehler - National Sales & Marketing Director

"I was impressed with the insights shown in this book that a person can take a lifetime to learn. Understanding faith as explained in the book shows how practical and necessary it is to lasting success, and confirms that absolutely anyone can change and adapt to make his or her life more meaningful and joyful."

Del Mecham - Manager of Provincial Hwy Condition Centre

"I feel a great warming comfort in understanding that all those feelings from within, which I have always experienced .... are actually affirmed & validated in this wonderful book - *FaithSkills* - Thank-you."

Simonne Bifolchi - Mother, Business Owner/Operator

More Real Results!

"I feel that your book really brings to the surface the spiritual side of life that is so real, yet often forgotten. *FaithSkills* really breaks down this side of our lives to the lowest common denominator giving us skills necessary to begin to function to our full potential."

Paul Jensen - President Cascade Wholesale

"*FaithSkills* is a shop manual for success. It has given me the diagnostic tools I needed to achieve the unrealized potential I had."

Harry Maylor - Master GM Technician

"In my opinion, this is a book you want to keep and always refer to for the rest of your life. It's refreshing to see that you can achieve success without giving up morality. It's truly different and practical. I found this book to be very validating."

Cathy Friesen, Professional Homemaker

"I loved the way the book uses simple skills to lay out a road map for your life to be built on faith, thus helping me to attain heights I never knew I was capable of. You find yourself nodding in agreement as you turn each page, and wondered why such simple truths were not revealed this way before."

Robert Kadlec - Father, Business Manager, Entrepreneur

"What a unique and refreshing view of inner faith! *FaithSkills* has given me a whole new perspective on self-development."

Vickie Terner - Mother, Author, Writer, Entrepreneur

"*FaithSkills* is an inspired work that is presented by a man who truly lives by faith. It has certainly given me the drive to take my efforts up to another level."

Michael Parker - Human Resources Dpt. Manager

"I love every story/illustration you presented. Some of them deeply touched me and brought me to a new understanding of people and the mechanics of relationships – parent-child, husband-wife, or just person to person. Lots of valuable stuff – pearls, as you call them in this book that will surely make someone a better person!"

Violy Mecham - Assistant Operations Manager

"I know I used to have a spirit when I was a child but I'd lost it. This has helped me find it again! If you've tried everything else this will definitely give you answers that other programs or books can't."

Stacey Granoff - Pennsylvania USA

ACKNOWLEDGEMENTS

"To The Women of My Life"

To my mother, Juliette Boisvert, who was an outstanding example of faith and endurance as she battled the demons of mental illness through the last semester of her life.

To Joanne, my wife, for the incredible example of humility she is to me. She perseveres to make life a success even though critical illness has robbed her of many of her prized skills and abilities.

To my sister, Simonne, whose diligent, caring nature always empowered me with the knowledge that I was not alone when difficulties were placed upon us as children.

To my sister, Yvonnette, who battles the ravages of a stroke in a way that amazes even those who care for her, but not us. Her example of determination has always fueled me to achieve.

To Debbie, my first wife, who at a very young age was an enormous example of courage to me by doing what she believed needed to be done, no matter how painful the results.

To my precious daughters, Christina and Jacklyn, who supported me and endured with me through the challenge of single parenthood. They both became beautiful rewards of parenthood, despite my shortcomings.

To my daughter, Emilie, my baby, the pearl of my eye. Her infectious giggle brightens my life and gives me joy by allowing me to be the child that the circumstances of my life didn't allow.

My deepest of thanks to Patricia (Trish) Sutton, my editor. She inspires and amazes me with her enormous skills with the written word and her keen ability to reason. Her possession of countless talents is only superseded by her humility to endure. Her faith is Incredible!

My profound appreciation for the patient, creative energy of my outstanding book designer Kami Morris.

Also, a Special Thanks to my summary editor, Melanie Reid, who in her soft, and professional way guided this work to a comforting conclusion.

In final acknowledgement, my gratitude goes to a young man in my life, my son Paul, who at age 9, made me more accountable than anyone else could have. His simple question -"Papa, have you sold any of your books yet?" - deeply motivated me to not only produce, but produce excellence, for him and others to cherish forever.

Table of Contents

Introduction

*Y*es, much to the amazement of others, I'd converted another lemon into lemonade. But this was not like the previous *success conversions* of my life, such as the ones where I'd transformed my severely dysfunctional upbringing into a stable, loving home life, or established a functioning family and business after my first wife ran off with my manager/friend and left me alone with two young daughters. Nor was it like when I converted early personal and business bankruptcy into internationally recognized success.

This time, it was different.

Armed with a PhD in Reality, my fourth business revival took place through the hands-on application of understandings that allowed me to literally design and manufacture the *success* my spirit desired. Step-by-step, I not only organized the environment, but did it with *authoritative passion.* My incredible zeal and confidence inspired the members of my new team to create another success faster than any other I'd previously achieved.

It was evident. Through reflection on my life's experiences, I'd finally understood the relationship between faith and success. I had gained the wisdom to apply the patterns necessary to actually *exercise faith in myself* sufficient to form the state of being that sage individuals, wise people who enjoy a fantastic quality of life, refer to as *permanent success*!

I had proven to myself, without a shadow of a doubt, that the Essential Foundations you're about to discover, when acted upon with *FaithSkills*, could fill absolutely anyone's critical fundamental needs. These are the primary and basic needs that act like roots; they drive all of our wants and needs.

Think about it. Isn't that what success is, a needs-filling process? Whether it's our own or someone else's, we're here to satisfy needs.

Every minute of our lives is needs-driven. I know it sounds a bit too simple to be true, but profound truths are always simple.

Seriously – go deep for a moment and reflect. Didn't you pick up this book to satisfy a need? I can assure you that *your spirit* did!

I wrote this book to help you not only recognize, but also understand, that parenting, business, marriage and just plain life are all exercises in faith. As you do, you will realize that trying to be successful at any one or all of these is usually counter-productive, because it leads to a life of frustration. Why? Because success is not an object we obtain or a destination we arrive at; as the word *successful* implies – it's actually a needs-filling process that's ever moving because we ourselves are progressive, and thus, so are our needs.

No wonder so many people are discouraged by trying to be *successful* – it's like trying to pin the tail on a moving donkey. Trust me, it's not a pretty sight; besides, you usually end up feeling like the ass when it's all over. Sound familiar? Been there, done that?

Well, that's about to change. By reading this book, you will reveal *the treadmill of successful* for what it really is, and possibly for the first time in your life, control success instead of the search for success controlling you. I can assure you that you will absolutely change the way you look at yourself – forever – and by so doing, immediately improve the world you live in.

Through the use of stories, I intend to introduce you to the process of *"proactive reflection."* It will assist you in realizing that you too have experienced the effects of the *currents* of your own powerful *fundamental needs* as they've pushed you from one dissatisfaction to another. You'll finally understand why satisfaction has often eluded you and that you're not the problem.

By discovering what Our *fundamental needs* are, you will learn to adapt *understandings* known as Essential Foundations, which are *doorways* between your spirit and your physical actions. They facilitate the sustained nourishment of your true and fundamental needs in ways that are constant and never changing.

Acting like prisms, Essential Foundations convert your every physical action into progressive, fundamental, needs-filling instruments for your spirit – that inner being that acts upon you and actually dictates whether you're satisfied or wanting. As a matter of fact, you will see as you read this book, that through the empowerment of your spirit, you will be able to restore, and even escalate, your zeal and passion for living the life you want, Today. You'll not only discover *what* to do, but *how* to do it, so it sticks!

By revealing the often-misunderstood skill of practical faith through a powerful skills set known as *FaithSkills*, you will facilitate your own progression from physical abilities to intellectual skills to faith-based talents. You will then effectively control your own destiny.

Your new level of awareness will reveal truths to your inner being that your spirit will absolutely recognize and your mind will intellectually verify. These truths will resonate as profound answers for those of you who are like me – sincerely motivated to *know from within* that you are entitled to get more out of life!

Come and be guided to actually *exercise faith in yourself* and make permanent positive changes in your life that produce concrete successes, permanent successes, that last. Come; restore your passion for life; and live like never before.

CHAPTER

1

The Pattern

At an early age, I recognized the powerful influence of patterns upon my quality of life. I wasn't fully aware that they were called patterns, but I knew their effects. They often consumed people to the point that their lives and the lives of others were deeply influenced – often in a negative way.

I think of my mom. She used to regularly sit down at the table in the early afternoon with her glass of tomato or orange juice (spiked with beer or vodka) and slowly drift off into lala land thinking we didn't know what was going on. When dinner time came, she boiled hamburger and served it to us in the *spirit* of healthy eating. Amazingly, I still like hamburger! Or, every fall and spring, as regular as clockwork, she would withdraw more and more into herself, responding to voices that only she could hear. As children, we were innocently witnessing the ravaging patterns of mental illness.

These and many other patterns influenced every aspect of my life – even the times that should have been happy, weren't. Take Christmas, for instance. Family feuds were typical. They erupted into grudges that were held for the remainder of the year – until the next round of *pleasurable drinking*. Not surprisingly, I've developed a deep disdain for alcohol.

Now, as I reflect, I can clearly see that it wasn't the alcohol itself that was the problem; it was ignorance of its natural pattern as well as a lack of self-discipline that allowed it to consume my family. Fortunately, both age and time help to change feelings. Our family, like many others, is wisely working on repairing the damaged relationships we have endured for most of our lives.

Yes, at an early age I learned to hope for better days, and quickly determined that I needed more than hope if I was to become a different person from the one that my surroundings dictated.

That's when I began searching for the so-called *secrets of success.* My brother in the city had become a millionaire; if he could do it, so could I.

So began my search for success, or money – they meant the same thing to me. What a ride. Made a fortune, lost a fortune. By age 29, I'd made a million all right – a million mistakes! I'd been bankrupt. My wife was gone. My 2 daughters and I were on our own. I was involved in a new business venture but didn't have a clue what I was doing. Even when I did get what I wanted, I realized that it wasn't really what I wanted. It seemed like I was continually completing the circle of stupidity through the skill of trial and error.

I had heard about and tried many programs that promised success, yet none of them focused on anything more than their own methods or particular points of view. There was nothing that explained how, and more importantly, why I needed to form successes. They all told me how to *think right* but rarely mentioned or considered how to *be right*.

Yet, I knew deep within myself that there had to be keys, constants that applied to anyone and everything. Why? Because I knew of so many different people with different approaches that were achieving enormous amounts of success. It wasn't until I filtered my knowledge through the analogy of baseball that I realized the nature of patterns and their relationship to the process of success.

Think for a moment.

We both know that in order for a run to count, a player has to touch the bases in a specific order – no exceptions. Now, there are different ways to accomplish this. You can hit a line drive and progress through the bases, or you can hit the ball off the center field wall. You most certainly don't have to bat it out of the park. As a matter of fact, you can even steal the bases, even home plate if you're good enough. But, regardless of your method, the same pattern still applies. You've got to touch all three bases in an order before you touch home plate so that a run can be a run.

Patterns are the game, but don't govern the game. Bases are

what the game is all about. No bases, no game. On the other hand, rules – such as you can't go to 3rd without touching 2nd – govern how we play the game. All those courses I took talked about the rules but not the patterns of success.

I further reflected on how Mother Nature provides the example of a perfect, self-governing pattern. As we try to understand its perfect pattern, we form rules that help us to relate it, and thus get the most out of it.

That's when I realized that real success, enduring success, must have a pattern, one as immovable and unchanging as the one found in Mother Nature. I now know that it does, and if it's used effectively, this pattern can empower anyone to act upon the certainties of life and so, form real and enduring successes. However, I have also discovered that if it is ignored, it will deliver the harsh reality of failure that ignorance so bountifully provides to the masses. I know, I used to belong to the masses.

The bottom line about patterns is this – master the pattern and you can master the laws. Master the laws and you can master the success you want – forever!

This chapter will explain the pattern used in this book that presents the pattern of permanent success. As you will see, it must be diligently followed so that your efforts (your runs) *count*.

I will also reveal to you the foundations, abilities, skills and talents that you need to apply in order to effectively utilize this pattern, but *please note*: it is very important for you to understand that I cannot tell you how to make this application; you must decide that for yourself.

That's what makes it so powerful.

Even though the pattern is the same for everyone, and can empower absolutely anyone, each person must create their own Personal Operating System within that pattern. It must be formed individually, for your unique life, so that it is worthwhile today and forever.

In the list below, we have explained the *key understandings* of this book's pattern. As you can see, these *understandings* are progressive in nature; they build one upon the other as do all things in the world of sage individuals.

- We have 7 *fundamental needs* that originate in our spirits, our inner beings, and can be fully satisfied through use of The Essential Foundations.

- The Essential Foundations are the missing links that act as *doorways* to connect our physical actions to our spirits.

- *FaithSkills* are talents developed through our understanding and use of the Essential Foundations.

- Develop *FaithSkills* and you begin to develop and exercise the skill of practical faith.

- Practical faith is discovered and enhanced through the skill of reflection, which helps you to experience and thus reveal these profound *understandings* or *foundations*.

- Everyone can adapt the pattern of a *FaithSkills* way of life and become empowered to build a life of *permanent success*.

The purpose of this book is to help *re-educate* you by demystifying the practical skill of faith, as I learned to do. You will learn how to actually use the elements of your innate success pattern. As you do, you'll ensure that your physical successes actually satisfy your spirit's fundamental needs, your *real* needs – the needs of your heart that actually drive every aspect of your life towards our common need to achieve. You will then be able to create *concrete, tangible* successes that have great worth to you. The result will be deep, personal fulfillment – success that not only creates, but perpetuates a life of constant fulfillment and joy.

How is this success pattern effectively implemented? Through the practical skill of faith.

Yes! Faith!

I know this may sound a bit bizarre to you but that's because we have effectively alienated ourselves from the discipline of faith. The common ways of the world have conditioned us to avoid the conscious exercise of faith's empowering and energizing skills.

However, if you think about it, you'll recognize that we unconsciously use it every day for simple tasks. For instance, when you got up this morning, didn't you exercise your spirit's will to alert your mind to act upon your body to *rise* to the day?

Absolutely!

That is the simplest, yet most critical use of faith. And for some, this real use of faith can be considered a miracle, considering the level of negativity that all too many allow themselves to live in. The fact is, we unknowingly and unconsciously use faith in every aspect of our lives.

Faith is like a candle. It can pierce the deepest and darkest parts of our lives. It is the very essence of self-esteem and the core of permanent success. If effectively used, it can allow us to rediscover, recognize and effectively apply our spiritual beings to our daily lives. We then can learn to have faith in ourselves and become empowered to satisfy the deep and powerful fundamental needs of our spirits and thus improve our quality of life forever.

You see, faith is absolutely required for any success to occur. Without it, *our will*, which comes from our spirit, cannot be manifested in this life and thus any attempt to respond to that *will*, or satisfy it, is impossible. Without basic faith, or even the unconscious use of it, we cannot satisfy any physical or spiritual need. Thus, we are unable to succeed. Just ask businesspeople or parents if they need to have faith in themselves in order for any sort of success to occur in their lives. More than others, they must have faith in themselves in order to even attempt to be what they've chosen to be.

However, because we've allowed religion to commandeer the word faith, and thus the discipline, we've unknowingly gone *underground* and thus become physically alienated from the invigorating force that is created from its conscious practical use. But slowly, we're becoming more aware of the influence our spirit can have on our own personal growth process. It's this prevalent self-awareness that is preparing so many to discover the immense power of faith and its relationship to our spirits and success – even *permanent success* – Here – Today – not in some other realm that many can't comprehend.

This book will act as a *road map* in helping you learn to navigate through this discovery process, which is why it is often referred to as *the owner's manual for success.*

We will use a story format to present this material. The stories are designed to cause you to reflect – to stimulate the relationship between your mind and spirit so you can reveal to yourself your innate skill of proactive reflection. You will see how you can empower yourself to change the circumstances of your life, may they be the culture of your business or the environment in your home.

Each story will be followed by a chapter that discusses the fundamental needs described in it and how each one was satisfied through applying one or more of The Essential Foundations through the talents of *FaithSkills*. These amazing talents will be introduced gradually throughout the book until you have studied all 13 of them and learned how they relate to The Essential Foundations.

Why this gradual introduction? *Because we want you to identify the clear association between the FaithSkills and their related foundations and how they must be combined to fill their associated fundamental need*. It's the individual, fundamental, needs-filling process that you must *first* learn to relate to. We will then guide you through the process required to individually develop these life changing *FaithSkills* talents so you, and those who surround you, can realize the amazing benefits of the powerful virtues they produce.

There are two chapters entitled *Sage Reflections*. These are meant to both summarize and clarify information discussed previously – *"you know, plan, do and review"*.

We've also placed *"focus boxes"* throughout the book, which are designed to stimulate unique, thought-provoking insights that help you understand how the principles apply in *real life* situations.

Time Out sections are also included throughout the chapters. Each one will be introduced by a *compass* symbol that looks like this: These are meant to encourage you to proactively reflect and discover new insights from the information we've presented you. As you do, you will form segways, or bridges, from understanding to understanding, that will reveal to your mind that you, too, are able to become sage about your life, as Webster defines it: "one who is wise from reflection and experience."

Is it time to awaken yourself and experience the quality of life that your inner being has been prompting you to create?

Is now the time for you to put *self* back into self-esteem and *be right*? In other words, to strive to become what your spirit knows it's meant to be?

If you answered *yes* to these questions, please accept my invitation to introduce you to the Essential Foundations of *permanent success* and the *FaithSkills* way of life. You will positively awaken yourself to personally *become* what your spirit's promptings and intuitions tell you is possible, and thus discover why you purchased this book.

Add color to the picture of your life by discovering what your heart really wants. Enrich your life with practical *understandings* and talents. Become what you're really meant to be!

A Permanent Success!

CHAPTER

2

Our Fundamental Needs

*E*arlier in my life, I was often described as a restless soul. I was never one to accept things as they are, so I regularly took charge of the undesirable circumstances in my life and changed them. Usually, I successfully achieved the results I desired. However, I would more often than not have a feeling of emptiness within me that could not be quenched by these constant goal-driven crusades I focused on in my leadership roles. You know, I was just like the dog that chases cars – frustrated once I caught one. And believe me – I caught many of them!

I am sure that many of you can relate!

It was reflection on this very circumstance that occupied my mind as I stepped on my cot so I could close the door to the storage room that now served as my bedroom. I was fighting for my very personal and financial existence – the nanny occupied the master bedroom and I couldn't afford to move to a larger home to get my own room. At least the storage room was comfy and dark and provided the privacy I needed to exercise faith in myself and Deity through prayer.

It was in one of those moments that I reflected and realized that I wasn't satisfying my innate needs. It was as if there was this different person within me that just wasn't happy with the life I was leading. Its goals and wants seemed the same as mine, or, at least, I thought they were, but I wasn't fulfilling them. I hadn't taken time to understand who or what that "other person" was and what his needs were.

Well, I am pleased to tell you that I now know the cause of the turmoil within me. I want to share with you what my discovery revealed to me and how it changed my life forever.

I discovered that no matter who we are, what we do, or what we believe, we all have 7 *fundamental needs* that must be satisfied

Rene Says

If you doubt that you have a spirit, do me a favor and close your eyes for a moment. Reflect and think back to a life-changing experience you've had. Can you not describe every detail to the point that you can actually hear the sounds, smell the scents and feel the emotions of the experience as if you were there again? Why is this so? Is it because your spirit was touched by the experience? Isn't that why you can recall it so clearly? Of course it is! That's why it changed your life. Whenever your spirit is touched, enormous changes can occur – often lifetime changes. Your mind

Continued next page...

in this life. Otherwise we feel confused, restless and unfulfilled by everything we do.

These needs come from our spirit. It is the inner being that drives all of us. Our spirit manifests its wants and needs in this life through what we call *our will*. Unless we physically meet our spirit's needs, they will become, or remain, restless.

That's why I was so restless. Like many of you, I hadn't discovered or accepted the influence of my spirit in my daily life. Thus I found myself constantly dissatisfied with the fruits of my labors, not only as a parent, or as a business owner, but in all other aspects of my life as well. It wasn't until I discovered and recognized what my true *fundamental needs* are, and where they originate, that I accepted the influence of my own spirit upon my life.

I can appreciate that this concept may be a new one for you, so let me open your awareness this way. Perhaps you speak a second language. You're out one day in a crowded place and suddenly you hear someone speaking your almost-forgotten native tongue. Your ears perk up, don't they? Or, if someone blurts out an old high school cheer that only a former student would know, not only are your ears aware, but

14

often, in moments of realization like these, your eyes will actually seek direct contact with the other person's eyes. It's a deep and often powerful recognition that takes place.

This deep feeling or recognition from within is your spirit's way of connecting to something familiar that exists in a different plane from the one in which you have the experience. If you allow it to, your spirit will manifest many such recognitions to your body in ways that are certain and often profound. No, you won't get struck by lightning, and I don't guarantee any apparitions. However, I can assure you that you will feel a deep sense of comfort that usually seems familiar.

Ever since I began this same discovery process that you're about to begin – and it all started with identifying and understanding these 7 *fundamental needs* – I have been able to create *permanent positive changes* within myself, and thus, create a life of *permanent success*.

No kidding. It was that simple. *Notice*: I didn't say easy – I said simple.

Now, before we get started, let me tell you that these needs will be presented in the order in which they must be satisfied for you to create permanent, enduring successes. You see, one builds upon the

Rene Says

never forgets the experience because it's written upon your living soul, which is the combination of your spirit and body. So now that you recognize the immense influence your spirit has upon your life, wouldn't it make sense to start living your life by the spirit? It's simple, but not easy. Just start to filter your thoughts through your spirit. Recognize the calmness and sense of peace that you feel. This is your spirit confirming the validity of your thoughts. You'll be amazed at how your confidence will grow as you develop this invigorating talent.

Go ahead –
Try it!

other. If we try to fulfill a need without addressing the previous needs, we frustrate our cause. It's like proposing marriage over your first cup of coffee – it just doesn't work! At least, not for me, but maybe for my cousin Pierre!

That's why a lot of people are disillusioned with many of the self-help processes they've tried. These processes don't create changes that last because they don't understand the need for order, let alone acknowledge that there is an order. They also don't identify nor understand the root, or cause, that forms the requirement for the skills and habits in the first place, so the new skill or habit is eventually frustrated. Why? Because it only deals with the behavior itself and not the *heart* of the behavior – you know – it doesn't satisfy the need that creates the behavior, often because a need is not understood to come from the spirit. Sadly, all too many people have given up on themselves because of this misdirection.

Our goal is to help you understand where these needs come from and how to satisfy them so you can avoid the frustrations mentioned above.

Let's begin.

The first of our Fundamental Needs is **Acceptance**.

Acceptance is one of our three *inward* needs that facilitate the growth of our inner being.

We all come into this life crying for acceptance and will all die yearning for it. We all want to be accepted in this world and there is absolutely nothing wrong with that! Someway, somehow, we all need to be wanted. The reason for this is that our *spirit* requires confirmation that it's at the right place – that it really belongs here.

There are varying degrees of meeting this need. The most superficial is through our *material* goods – our position in life, our money, our possessions – are necessary to provide benefits to those whose attention or affection we crave.

Then there is a deeper degree, which is *knowing* that we are actually liked. This means that the spirit of another person has acknowledged us.

Lastly, there is the *supreme* fulfillment of this need, which is the complete and unconditional acceptance of our spirit by another spirit, which we understand as true love. You see, before we came here, our spirits were all together; we were completely accepted for who we were. Our spirits yearn to duplicate that feeling – it is a real and genuine need.

Acceptance is the very *root* of self-esteem.

So profound is this need for acceptance, that it literally preoccupies all of our physical life on this earth. It is the need that must be addressed first, or at least *be in progress* and eventually satisfied, or any and all attempts to satisfy other needs will be futile.

So instinctive is this need that many become consumed by it, but unfortunately they omit to address the root of this need, which is the requirement of their spirits to be accepted or esteemed. That is why so many are frustrated in their efforts to build their self-esteem.

If you doubt what I say, ask yourself – ask your spirit – is this true? Ponder for a moment on this question: "Do I, or my actions or efforts, need to be accepted in order for me to be able to accept myself, and thus gain a sense of purpose in my life?"

I hope that you felt a sense of calm, a kind of "yes, that makes sense" feeling that actually seems familiar to you.

As a matter of fact, it may even seem like *common sense.*

That's because it is common to you. It's knowledge that comes from the common intelligence we all possess, and your spirit recognizes it. In other words, it's spiritually familiar!

Remember – if you allow it to, your spirit will always recognize truths about itself! Spiritual facts support themselves.

> **Think about it**
>
> What's Common Sense? Why is it called common when it is so hard to find? Because it's intelligence that our spirits recognize. It's not common because our minds haven't converted it to knowledge yet. That's why there's nothing common about common sense! Make Sense?

The Second Fundamental Need is **Knowledge**.

Knowledge is the second of our three *inward* needs. We all have an incredible thirst for knowledge. We not only need to know that we are accepted here on this earth, but we also need to know *why* we're here. Everyone of us has a burning desire to understand our purpose in this life.

You see, our spirit knows there is a purpose for everything, but because it's unfamiliar with this dimension – physical life – it satisfies this *fundamental need* through you asking the question WHY!

The word WHY is the root of all knowledge; knowledge is the physical manifestation of the common intelligence we all possess. In other words, knowledge is the result when our spirit translates intelligence into this dimension – physical life. We are here to gain knowledge and our spirits thirst for it – constantly!

The Third Fundamental Need is **Harmony**.

Once we've discovered acceptance and knowledge, our first and second *inward* needs, doesn't it seem natural that we would want to satisfy them in ways that would last?

Of course it does! Permanence – stability – is what we crave!

Thus, we must satisfy the third of our *inward* needs – harmony. It provides comfort. Harmony is also the very essence of permanence.

Harmony is achieved when we have balance, which is learned by facing and overcoming opposition.

The sooner we understand the need for opposition in achieving balance and harmony, the sooner we can act upon that opposition, thereby gaining a sense of purpose, not confusion, from our conflicts.

The Fourth Fundamental Need is **Identity**.

So, now that we know that it is natural, even necessary, for us to have difficulties in our physical quest to attain harmony, we arrive at the next natural need: for whom is this harmony being achieved?

> **Think about it**
>
> How could you appreciate black if you didn't have white? How would you know good if you had never experienced bad? Balance needs opposition to exist! Without it, balance is not only unnecessary, it's impossible.

In other words, who are you? What makes you? How does your spirit relate to you and the process of fulfilling your needs?

You will discover that you are a spirit in a physical body, discovering an intelligence that you already possess. We are here in this dimension – physical life – to discover and improve our individual beings by affirming our innate spiritual abilities and capacities in order to further expand upon them. As we do so, we will reveal other skills and talents that we possess but couldn't comprehend because they required this dimension – mortal, physical life – in order to manifest themselves. This whole process is part of what we often refer to as *building a character*.

As you learn to recognize that you are a spirit in a physical body, discovering the intelligence that you already possess, you are satisfying the *stabilizing* need in your life – the need for identity.

> **Think about it**
>
> Where do *natural* talents come from and why are they called *natural*? Is it because they come from within? If so, where does *within* come from? Is it possible that we had a previous identity? Could it be that we're here in these physical bodies to discover what that previous existence we call *natural*, really is?

Why is this important? Because once you know who you are, you have a strength from within that allows you to better satisfy your three *outward fundamental needs*. It also helps you to appreciate the magnitude and importance of this life. You will realize that you are totally empowered to literally become all that you desire to become. *Your potential is literally unlimited.*

Please note: your capacity to satisfy this need is only sufficient once the process of *satisfying your inward needs* is understood and undertaken.

Address your inward needs first and your need for identity will become evident for you to satisfy.

The Fifth Fundamental Need is **Direction**.

Our spirits yearn to satisfy our need for direction, the first of our three *outward* needs – those that are satisfied by relating our inner being with the world we live in so we can move forward in achieving our goals. We long for answers to the *how* of fulfilling our purposes in this life. Once we ask *why*, we immediately ask *how*; that's perfectly natural – it's what our spirits need.

You see, our spirits know that we're here for specific purposes; they want to discover the elements that direct this dimension – physical life – in order to achieve those goals! They need to know the *rules of the game* so to speak.

Our spirits know that it's no different now than it was before; laws and/or patterns govern creation. They yearn to know how to apply our three-dimensional beings to these patterns in order to satisfy the need for direction.

Remember – your spirit already knows that every success you achieve is the direct and relevant result of applying the pattern, or adhering to the law that governs it; it just needs to know which direction to take in implementing these laws.

Think about it

Why are most of us uncomfortable when we are lost? When we lose our *sense* of direction, why do we innately strive to regain it? Could it be that our inner being knows that everything has an order, and that there's a *path* for everything?

Could we pause for a Sage Moment?

Now that you've progressed 2/3 of the way through this chapter, let's reflect for a moment upon what we've shared up to now.

1. We need **Acceptance** – confirmation that we belong here.
2. We need **Knowledge** – knowing why we're here.
3. We need **Harmony** – stability in what we're doing here.
4. We need **Identity** – understanding who we are in this dimension and how we relate to it.
5. We need **Direction** – understanding the laws and patterns that govern this life and how we use them to relate to this dimension.

Take a moment to compare what you've just read with the experiences of your life. Does this material make sense? Does it cause you to have feelings inside? What kinds of feelings? Do they affirm to you that the needs we've explained are indeed the ones that have been driving your spirit?

Rene Says

This physical life is unfamiliar to our spirits, thus they need to discover and understand the patterns of life in order to have direction. The examples of others will often provide patterns. Set the example and others will often follow, especially if your example touches them to the core. It is for this precise reason that in many societies the positions of parenting and business ownership are held in high regard. While in these offices of life, one's actions are observed as examples or patterns for those for whom

Continued next page...

The Sixth Fundamental Need is **Empowerment**.

Empowerment is the second of our three *outward* needs. Our spirits must have their need for empowerment satisfied if we are to be successful. This occurs when our spirit applies its will on our lives. This freedom to choose whether or not to obey life's laws and patterns is known as agency.

We must be empowered to exercise agency upon our lives. It is the ultimate reason for being here. It is fundamental to our existence. Past and present wars indicate that whenever this freedom has been threatened, we are willing to fight to the death to maintain it.

We must be personally empowered to make this life of worth to us. We need to be able to fulfill our purpose to develop our self-identities in order to progress according to our wills. It is also important to recognize that we must use our agency to obey life's natural laws and patterns if we wish to be empowered by them.

True empowerment can only occur when our spirits' will is enacted through our physical action, which is why we need to understand our spirits' needs versus our body's wants.

The Seventh Fundamental Need is **Fulfillment**.

Fulfillment is the third of our three *outward* needs. In a recent survey undertaken by our Academy, 75% of respondents believed "that we are innately programmed to succeed." We must not only succeed in this life, but we must also be fulfilled by our successes in this life. Fulfillment is the very essence of permanent success. Yes, permanent success is possible. As a matter of fact, it's the ultimate reason for this journey we call life.

As we form our own patterns through the patterns of life, and achieve goals that fulfill our 7 *fundamental needs*, we form a character, a strong spirit if you will, that exudes virtues that can influence the lives of others. Our spirits know that we are not here to fail, as many of the skeptics and pundits of this world would have us believe. Our spirits know that just being here is a success!

Our spirits also know that we are here to have joy. It's this innate knowledge that "fuels" the hope we all have. Hope, the pure energy of our spirits, is the motivator that drives us to attain joy. Joy is deep. It's happiness that keeps giving

Rene Says

one is responsible. Both offices are demanding and difficult, but incredibly rewarding and empowering when approached with a person's best efforts. Sadly, too many either aren't aware of this, or deny the mantle that these privileged opportunities offer, thus they diminish the impact that parenting and business ownership should have. So, if you're a parent or an entrepreneur or both, try exampling the behaviors you would like to see your team members have, then watch them rise to the occasion – especially teenagers! I know it's hard to believe, but they yearn for mentors.

23

because it's happiness on a spiritual plane.

When you recognize and identify your *fundamental needs* and begin the process of fulfilling them, you start to have joy –

- JOY that comes from a sure knowledge that you belong here and that you have a purpose;

- JOY from knowing that the obstacles and challenges you have are for your own good – they're necessary in order to create balance in this life;

- JOY that comes from knowing that you're a spirit in a body with the sole purpose of discovering the immense intelligence that you already possess in order to not only affirm but also enhance who you really are;

- JOY that comes from the manifestation of your ability to observe the eternal and practical laws of this life;

- JOY that comes from knowing that what you're doing in this life, at this time, is right for you, and that the people who surround you are the right people to assist you in meeting your needs.

Does this feel possible to you?

Remember, you can achieve whatever you set your spirit to!

Again, I ask you to filter what you've just read through your spirit. Form the question in your mind, ask it, and then wait for your feelings – the communicators of your spirit – to tell you if it's true. Recognize the calm and comfort you feel. That feeling is your spirit confirming the validity of what you've just read.

Realize that your spirit acts upon you much like the wind does upon the trees. You can't see it, but you can feel it and see its effects. When you understand this, you'll discover what the skill of faith does. Faith is the power that directs the force of your spirit to act upon your body, or in other words, your physical life. By directing your body, you can use the force of the invisible wind to act upon you positively, much like the wind does with a kite. It's a practical skill that is totally misunderstood by many people today so don't feel uninformed.

Faith is much more than a religious term. It's a learned skill that empowers your spirit to act upon your life and thus fulfill your *fundamental needs,* or, in other words create permanent enduring successes.

As you recognize and understand the relationship of your intelligence, spirit, and body you will begin to harness this invigorating practical skill. And yes, faith is practical. It is only when faith is practically applied, can it convert from a skill to a power. All too many concentrate on the latter and forget the practical application which is why faith has been so misunderstood. It is only through the practical use of faith that you can gain real power over your life.

Rene Says

Success building is much like learning to drive a standard vehicle. You need to understand the need for a clutch and how to use it. If you don't, you'll never be able to appreciate its main benefit – control of the vehicle. You see, you're much like the Formula One Series race cars – you're not only built to reach incredible rates of speed, you're designed to have control over your life. Just as a driver has ultimate control of enormous amounts of horsepower when he or she uses a sophisticated clutch, so you can empower your success building process with an awareness of your powerful clutch – your spirit. As you discover the source of this horsepower – your *fundamental needs* – you'll be able to successfully navigate an invigorating victory in this exciting race we call life!

Here is a summary of the *fundamental needs*.

ACCEPTANCE
(We need to Belong)

KNOWLEDGE
(We need to Know Why)

HARMONY
(We need Comfort)

IDENTITY
(We need to know Who we are)

DIRECTION
(We need to know How)

EMPOWERMENT
(We need to Exercise our Wills)

FULFILLMENT
(We need to Achieve)

Pro-Active Reflection

Now that you've discovered *your fundamental needs*, examine the tapestry of your memory through these new understandings. Use your spiritual glasses and look into the rear view mirror of your life. Do you see that the most significant, the most colorful, of those memories are ones that were woven by your spirit? They were woven with the threads of these needs. Whenever your spirit was touched through the fibres of these needs, a memory was immediately woven to hang on the walls of your mind. *Try this*: Close your eyes and retrieve the thoughts of your mind through your spirit and enter the gallery of those life-changing experiences. As you will undoubtedly re-experience them, because your spirit was involved, you will see how the weaving of your needs was involved: for example, when you may have been severely disciplined and really wondered if you belonged – acceptance and direction or when you achieved a long sought-after goal. Isn't it amazing how we can so easily recall those moments of graduation – knowledge, identity, empowerment, achievement, fulfillment. Or, the ultimate memory, when you knew you were in love. That moment when your spirit was totally and unconditionally accepted for what it was. Awesome memory, isn't it? I definitely treasure that one because all of my needs were totally fulfilled. Weren't yours? Absolutely nothing else mattered, did it?

Now, go ahead. Empower yourself for the future by further examining and recognizing the impact that the fulfillment of your spirit's fundamental needs has had on your life to date. As you do, your capacity to weave a magnificent tapestry of joy, real joy, is greatly enhanced. By strategically fulfilling your spirit's fundamental needs through your future daily actions with the new *FaithSkills* talents you're about to discover, and hopefully assimilate, you will ensure yourself of a life of enduring success, even *permanent success*! So, now that you know how to proactively reflect, make sure that you use the proactive reflection boxes that we've provided at the end of every chapter. They're there to trigger you to harness the instantaneous power of revelation through reflection.

Do it. You won't regret it!

Pro-Active Reflection

CHAPTER

3

The Missing Link

I'm sure you'll agree that there's nothing like real experience to teach you the lessons of life. Usually it involves a lot of emotions that cause a great deal of turmoil, but the lesson is learned forever and contributes to one's level of wisdom. I, for one, have found that these profound moments of growth are often facilitated when a new level of understanding has been gained or vaulted upon us by our circumstances. I call these, *"ah-ha,"* moments.

For me, the most profound of these occurs when seemingly insignificant, concrete actions reveal or fulfill major intangible needs. Think of this in terms of family life. When I do the dishes for my wife without being asked, offer to take the kids for the afternoon, or simply open the door for her even though we've been married for years, I prove to her that she has value to me. This, in turn, earns me her loyalty and respect for the times when I need it. And trust me, I have a strong need for a cheerleader – Joanne's the best!

I've also learned from other experiences about the relationship between tangible actions and intangible needs. Several years ago, a "good" friend and business partner taught me the hard way.

We had just come off several *rocking* years in business; awards were plentiful and cash flow was healthy. I decided that it was time to grow, not only for my own benefit but also for the benefit of my prized manager. So, when one of those *deals of a lifetime* opportunities for expansion presented itself, I jumped on it.

I talked to my manager and told him that if he could achieve the same level of profits we'd made together, but do it without my hands-on involvement, for five years, I'd give him 50% of the shares of the crown jewel outlet. No capital was required of him, just pure sweat equity.

Well, things rolled on for a year as I revived the newly obtained outlet. But I began to wonder why sales were dropping and profits were dwindling, yet the manager wasn't worried. When I questioned him about the situation, he gave me a nebulous response. Then a few months later, there was a request for a raise in pay. I was stunned. I simply reminded him that he was in control of his destiny as a partner; he determined his take-home pay through a lucrative bonus plan that I hadn't removed, even though he became a partner with shares in escrow.

Well, a few months went by. There was no increase in profits nor did the bonus occur, yet there was no more complaining. I wondered why the wheel had stopped squeaking without any grease. I had my suspicions. They were fueled by two incidents. I was in the office one afternoon and witnessed him misleading a customer with an outright lie, and then overheard him speaking with his wife on the phone and telling her a blatant lie, even though I was right there and could hear every word he said.

That's when my *spidey senses* recognized a missing link. My complete inner being was alerted. I thought: "If he's willing to lie to his wife, he'll lie to anyone, so what makes me think he won't lie to me?"

Even though he had been with me 7 years, I couldn't deny the reality of what my mind told me. He didn't understand the Essential Foundation of Commitment. He wasn't faithful to his wife, the #1 person that deserved his faithfulness, so why would I be naïve enough to think he would be faithful to me, let alone be trustworthy.

My heart was wrenched, yet I couldn't deny the logic of what was happening. Then it really hit me. For years I had seen him mess around with me and others over small issues requiring his word. Many times I caught him telling little "white lies".

How stupid it was of me to think that he would mature or change just because I'd placed a mantle of trust upon him. He had proven that he didn't have the vaguest understanding of the essential requirement of trust, nor of faithfulness, in building a relationship. The only thing he was good at was being present. His life was purely physically based, yet I was expecting him to live a higher standard simply by putting him into a situation that required it. It didn't work. He needed to create it himself from within.

Well, I decided to validate my new revelation and test the man's integrity – I wanted to be sure so I seeded the cash box. The money disappeared. But, I wanted to give him the benefit of the doubt, so I did it for three more weeks. Sadly, all the extra cash that didn't have a known work order or receipt attached was gone. Reality really hit me hard.

Remember This

Essential means absolutely necessary. Foundation means based on or supported by. Sounds like pretty good stuff to have, doesn't it?

Needless to say, life changed after this awakening experience. I learned that the seemingly unimportant actions that relate to trust must never be tampered with in any shape, form or manner. I now clearly understood the relationship between physical actions and intangible needs. It was a rude awakening!

You may have had similar experiences. Hopefully, they won't be repeated in the future because this book will teach you how to adopt and utilize The Essential Foundations in your life so you know how to orchestrate successes, not disappointments. When you gain clear understandings of elements of this life that can govern your physical actions in fulfilling intangible needs, you will discover a *doorway* that can form an essential foundation.

The purpose of this chapter is to introduce you to The Essential Foundations, often referred to as the "True North" of the sage world because of their constant, stabilizing forces. Just as a metal link can join two separate pieces of chain and convert them into a powerful tool, so can these Essential Foundations link your *fundamental needs* to your *FaithSkills*.

These foundations are sometimes referred to as *understandings*. They are the intersections where intelligence, body and spirit connect. It is here that *understandings* become beliefs that are

Rene Says

The key to living by the spirit is communing with your spirit. You do this by physically stimulating your mind so your spirit can access and form your thoughts to influence the actions of your body. Indirectly, that's what occurs through the process of hypnosis. Fortunately, you can do this consciously by examining your behaviors to determine your own personal access points. For me, it's the shower, or a long drive in a familiar car. Both of these activities act upon my physical body and occupy my brain while stimulating and comforting both at the same time. While this is happening, my

Continued next page...

then expressed through actions. My manager's actions clearly displayed his beliefs, and thus the level of his *understandings*. Unfortunately, at the time, his wife didn't recognize this. Neither did I. Or, maybe we just didn't want to admit the truth.

I hope you won't be like my manager, or naïve like me. You won't, if you adopt these new *understandings* into your *auto pilot* behavior. Your actions will radiate a deep inner confidence, a *spiritual confidence* if you will, that will clearly tell others that you've "got it together". You will be recognized as one who has strong leadership skills because you not only *"talk the walk"* you *"walk the talk"*.

However, one must clearly understand that the empowerment and permanence of these foundations occurs only when they are built upon each other in the correct order. *There are no shortcuts here.* If you ignore these important facts, be prepared for failure. You will literally be building your house of success on sand – we all know that's not a wise choice!

Now, at this point you may be wondering if we are preparing you to be a duplicate, a clone, of every other individual seeking to make *permanent positive changes* in his or her life. We're not! As we explained in Chapter One, our goal is to help you understand the patterns that lead to enduring successes so you can then use them in your own way to form your *FaithSkills* Personal Operating System – one that meets your needs. It will most likely be quite different from the systems developed by others.

Now, let's talk about the way we've structured the following chapters that introduce and discuss the Essential Foundations. We hope that the organization we've used will facilitate your assimilation of the material into your life in a way that has value to you.

It's important to note that we have presented the Essential Foundations in specific categories. These not only reflect their "natures" as interpreted in the physical world in which we live, but also the way they will evolve for you as you implement these foundations into your *auto-pilot* of behaviors and form your own *FaithSkills* Personal Operating System.

Thus, as you discover these categories you will see that they too exhibit how understandings must be built one upon the other in order for them to have stability.

Rene Says

mind races away and is easily spoken to by my spirit. Nothing is more invigorating to me than a long drive or a 1-hour shower. Talk about getting re-energized. For some, music has a similar influence, while hiking does the trick for others. That's also why nature can be so soothing yet stimulating. Our physical bodies are in familiar surroundings and our minds are free to commune with our spirits. Discover a physical behavior that energizes you in the same way. I call this *conscious hypnosis.* Try it! You'll be amazed to discover the wonderful spirit you really are and the amazing power it can have upon your life - TODAY!

The Essential Foundations are categorized as follows:

• the **fundamental** foundations: organization, order and purpose – they satisfy our *inward fundamental needs* for Acceptance and Knowledge;

• the **leveling** foundations: balance and opposition – they meet our *inward fundamental need* for Harmony;

• the **identifying** foundations: intelligence, body and spirit – they meet our *stabilizing* Need for Identity;

• the **empowering** foundations: law, agency and action – they satisfy our *outward fundamental needs* for Direction and Empowerment;

• the **resulting** foundation: the harvest – it partially fills our *outward fundamental need* for Fulfillment; and lastly,

• the **governing** foundation: commitment – it completes our *outward fundamental need* for Fulfillment

We will present the Essential Foundations and their accompanying *FaithSkills* in the order of these categories as stated above. We do so in the form of parables, or stories, so you can not only relate with them but also consider how they can apply to your life. Each story will present a combination of characters – parents, businessmen, sailors, etc. Some are just learning about the Essential Foundations, their associated *FaithSkills*, and how to implement them, while others already know how to use them effectively and are teaching others.

The chapter following each case study will analyze what happened in the story and also help you put yourself into it so you can *experience* the situation in *your own way*. We hope this will assist you in *assimilating* the information unto yourself.

We will present each Essential Foundation with its associated

FaithSkill. We are doing so in order for you to *clearly understand the relationship that the FaithSkill has to the Essential Foundation and the fundamental need it fulfills. It is important that you understand these relationships in order to better absorb and assimilate the process of building and mastering these FaithSkills as presented in detail in Chapter 19.*

To further assist in this process of relating the Essential Foundations to their associated *FaithSkills* , we have included *"Pro-Active Reflection"* boxes at the end of each chapter so you can record any thoughts that come to your mind as you read. As you write down these often rapid and unexplained thoughts, you will introduce yourself to the process of personal reflection, which will help this book become the revelatory experience it is intended to be.

We've also placed boxes within the review chapters to allow you to write your immediate answers to questions that we hope will facilitate your active participation, and thus rapid immersion, into these new understandings.

As you learn from the stories how to implement these Essential Foundations, you will be empowered to effectively exercise *FaithSkills* at will. This will allow you to harness the power of your spirit in your daily actions so you can *Live your life by the spirit.* When you do this, immense and powerful changes occur – it is literally how you can *move the mountains of your life.*

There is a lot of new information in this book, thus we hope that you will take time to not only review the material, but also to reflect upon it. I've been told "this book needs to be kept close at hand as a constant reference manual" – we hope it will become such a resource for you.

Now, before we close this discussion, I want to verify why we've taken this chapter to present the categories, or natures of these foundations. "There is a season for all things." It's no different than multi-tasking as a business owner/operator or a parent. Apply the wrong skill or understanding at the wrong time and disaster is sure to occur. Try selling a customer your services when you're still wearing the *"production hat"*. It just doesn't happen. You're trying to instill confidence in the customer, while at the same time, your mind is racing because you're wondering how the crew in the back is potentially messing up. Or, try wearing the *"checkbook hat"* when you're striving to inspire your child as you help with homework. You're just not there, *and that's not a good thing.*

You need to apply the correct skills, talents and abilities to the task at hand or else your juggling routine is doomed for injury! That's what happened to my manager. He thought the "key" was juggling, when in fact, it was to know what and when to juggle. Since our partnership had satisfied his physical need, he relaxed his guard and continued to perform his juggling routine with people's trust. All he was doing was manipulating, juggling us like he had all the other issues he *managed* in his life. Some things just aren't meant to juggle – trust being one of them.

We don't want this fiasco to happen to you and it won't, if you understand these Essential Foundations by their categories and assimilate them accordingly into your life. You'll move from one positive experience to another.

So now that we're both on the same page, take a look at the following chart to review what we've discussed. Then, on to the stories. Enjoy!

The Category Their Physical "Natures"	The Essential Foundation (s)	The Fundamental Need
GOVERNING	Commitment	FULFILLMENT
RESULTING	The Harvest	
EMPOWERING	Action	EMPOWERMENT
	Agency	
	Laws	DIRECTION
IDENTIFYING	Body	IDENTITY
	Spirit	
	Intelligence	
LEVELING	Opposition	HARMONY
	Balance	
FUNDAMENTAL	Purpose	KNOWLEDGE
	Order	
	Organization	ACCEPTANCE
This type of	Foundation satisfies	this need

Pro-Active Reflection

CHAPTER

4

The Rude Awakening

*A*s Cameron trudged home from school in the pouring rain, it was all he could do to hold back the tears. This has been the absolute worst day of my life, he thought. Why me?

For a split second, he allowed his mind to think back on his math class at 1:40 that afternoon. That's when his nightmare had started – exactly at that moment in time.

He knew he hadn't done that well on the test, but he reminded himself that he had tried, and at least should have passed. As the paper slid off the desk into his lap, he took a sideways glance at the mark. 26 out of 80. It couldn't be. He looked again at the numbers staring at him from the page. It was true. 26 out of 80. Five light strokes of a red pen had sealed his fate. He was a failure.

His stomach churned as he walked out of one deep puddle into another. The sound of his boots dragging through the water weighed on his heart. I'm not going to think about it anymore he told himself. If I do, I'll be sick.

As the wind picked up and blew relentlessly around him, his hands began to feel cold from the stinging droplets of rain. His mind raced. Maybe I should run away from home. I could stay up in the tree house for a few days – no one would think to look for me there. No one would even care to look. Who would want a failure like me in their family? Maybe I could throw the test into the garbage can beside the fence – no one would know.

Oh, no! My parents – they'll kill me. Mom warned me this would happen if I didn't pay more attention. But to what? How was I supposed to know? Math was beyond me. My scrambled brain just didn't get it. Besides all that, why do I need to know math anyway? It's just a bunch of stupid numbers. I can't do it. I don't want to do it. I'm not going to do it.

For a moment, that last thought made him feel powerful – but only for a moment. Then grim reality set in. No matter which way he thought about it, the horrible numbers didn't lie – 26 out of 80. He was still a failure. The tears began to flow freely.

Angela looked up as she heard the screen door slam. There he goes again, she thought. Why can't ten-year-olds just close the door like everyone else? Why do they have to slam it? She began to deliver lecture 48 – the one about not slamming doors – when Cameron poked his head around the corner. Angela knew instantly that this was not the time for a lecture about doors.

He was a mess. Muddy shoes. Wet shirt. No coat. Stringy hair. But it was his face that worried her. His red, swollen eyes told the whole story. What on earth had happened?

He just stood there, staring at her.

"Do you want to talk, son?"

He hesitated, then fell into her arms. She hugged him. He cried, then tried to talk, then cried some more. Cameron had totally crashed. His heart was heavy with a deep sense of hopelessness. Math had defeated him and he knew it.

Slowly, the sobbing and crying stopped.

"Oh, Mom, I'm stupid. I'm a doughhead. I can't do math. I won't ever be able to do it. I'm a failure just like that ugly duckling in the story you used to read to me. What am I going to do?" wailed Cameron. He poured out his heart to his mother, as only a defeated child can – the whole embarrassing, frustrating story, injury upon injury.

As a devoted parent, Angela's heart went out to him, yet an encouraging feeling came over her. She had been trying for months to help Cameron; he wouldn't let her. But now? Much as she hated to see her son in such a state, she realized that finally, the all too familiar *"teachable moment"* had arrived.

"Why don't you go and clean up a bit – put on some dry clothes and wash your face. Then I have something to show you."

You see, Angela was an accomplished student in the school

of life. She had learned that if there comes a time when humility can replace stubbornness, an opportunity for learning occurs. On several occasions, Angela's older sister Rita, her surrogate mother, had utilized such key moments to teach her some of life's necessary lessons. She realized that now was the time for her to do the same for her son.

Cameron returned to the kitchen a few minutes later. Angela had finished cooking the macaroni for the dinner casserole, and was now preparing to make some chicken noodle soup, a Mother's bullet-proof pacifier.

She peered out the window to see the dull effect the rain was having upon the day. Calmly she said, "I'd like to talk a little bit about water."

Water? thought Cameron. What's that got to do with anything?

"Where do we get water, Cam?" asked Angela, as she poured the soup mix in the pot.

"Just look outside, Mom, there's enough out there for a year."

Angela looked at him with that "Okay, you're witty" look that only a mother can deliver, and said, "Seriously, there's more to it than that."

He thought for a minute. "Well, it rains, like it is today. The water stays in puddles, lakes and oceans, then it evaporates, makes clouds, it rains again – you know, that whole water cycle thing. Mrs. Kennedy made us learn that stuff in science class."

"Obviously, you learned it well," said Angela. "You see, school does have a purpose."

Cameron groaned.

"Now," continued Angela, "did you consider that water needs to be organized in order to make use of it?"

"Organized? You mean like the clothes in my drawers?" A typical sarcastic statement – Cameron was on his way back.

"Not quite. I was thinking more of this. How is the rain that is pouring down today eventually going to come out of my tap here at the sink?"

"Oh," said Cam, "you mean like a bunch of pipes to bring the water from up there into our houses. They need to be good ones so that stuff doesn't get stuck in there and stop the water from moving. I hope they keep them clean too – I sure don't want to drink dirty water."

"You're right, Cam. All of those things need to be considered when organizing the water for our use. Now, can you see how this idea of organization can apply to your math?" asked Angela.

Cameron thought for a minute. Math and water? Together? No way. Water's cool – math isn't.

Angela interrupted his thoughts. "Think about this. When we want to have running water in our house, what has to happen?"

"We need to turn on the tap?" quipped Cameron mischievously.

Angela rolled her eyes.

"OK, OK. I suppose we need to gather it up into those big reservoirs we saw last summer."

"That's correct. Then?"

"Somebody has to put pipes in the ground so the water can come into the house."

"That's right, but don't the workers have to know what they're doing and why they're doing it before they start moving dirt to put those pipes in the ground?"

"Yeah, but what's that got to do with math?"

"There are lots and lots of numbers out there, but math involves organizing them in certain ways for certain purposes. For instance, when you want to add numbers, you've already learned that you need to put them together – like what we do when we gather large volumes of water in those reservoirs. When you subtract, you need to take something away, which is what the workers do when they put the pipes in the ground – they remove dirt."

"Oh," said Cam slowly. "And when you multiply, you organize numbers into groups and put them together to get an answer. When you divide, you separate them into groups to get an answer."

"Exactly," continued Angela. "When we organize numbers, we get useful information. When we organize water, it also works for our benefit. If you organize it correctly, it can become useful in lots of ways – like making this bowl of soup."

She now had Cameron's complete attention.

"Order is also a very important thing to remember when we use water. Do you remember what I was doing when you first walked into the kitchen?"

"You were yelling at me about not slamming the door," said Cam.

Angela looked sheepish – she really should have let him come in before she started talking – then she would have known not to mention the door. Next time, she thought. Next time, I'll look first.

"That's OK, Mom. You've told me a million times not to slam that door. Anyway, I think you were cooking macaroni," said Cam.

"Right. How do you think order applies to that process?"

"You need to boil the water first, then add the macaroni so it will cook. If you tried to cook the macaroni first, and then add the water, what a mess!"

The confident tone was returning to his voice.

"Absolutely!" Angela joyfully affirmed. "Now…"

Cam interrupted. "I know what you're going to say. Order is also important in math. Like when I do that order of operations thing. I have to figure out the answers in the right order, otherwise, the whole thing is wrong. Or, like positive and negative numbers. When I'm adding them, I have to go in a certain order or I get the wrong sign and the wrong number."

"That's right, Cam. We organize numbers into certain orders so we get useful numbers that give us answers to our questions, such as how much water is needed in the pot to cook enough macaroni for dinner tonight."

Angela noticed that Cam's facial expression had changed.

He was no longer as anxious and frustrated as he had been at the beginning of their conversation. Hope had replaced fear. There was just one more thing she had to help him understand.

"OK, Cam, now tell me what you've learned so far."

"Water needs to be organized so it can come out of the tap in our house. I sometimes need to use it in a certain order with other stuff, or it won't do what it's supposed to do. Numbers need to be organized so I can figure out what to do with them. They also need to be used in order sometimes to get the right answers. If you put them where they belong....gee, Mom, maybe math isn't as scary as I thought. Maybe I can do it."

Angela's smile spread slowly across her face. Pay dirt, she thought. Finally, a chance to clarify principles that he already knows, but didn't recognize or know how to use.

"One last thing," exclaimed Angela. "I think I know the roadblock that's kept you from learning math. There's something called purpose. Both water and math can be used to achieve certain purposes."

"No kidding," said Cameron, sarcastically. "You mean that math actually has a purpose other than making me feel stupid?"

"Yes, it does, my son, but when you understand this last important item, you won't feel like that anymore."

"Now," said Angela, "let's go back to the water issue for a minute. Other than cooking macaroni, what other purposes does it have?"

"Cleaning things, drinking, washing clothes and dishes and cars."

"True. Now, think about this. Do we sometimes change its form to make it serve our purposes?"

"I guess we do," admitted Cam. "We make it into ice to keep our juice cold. Oh, yeah, and when you iron my shirt, you pour water into the iron to make steam so you can smooth out the wrinkles. It wouldn't work if you just used water by itself."

"Right. Numbers are used in different forms and for different purposes too. When you understand that, you'll want to use them more often. Remember when we bought that new bed for you last week? I wrote a check to pay for it. Why would math be helpful to me then?"

"I dunno. I thought you just wrote a check whenever you wanted something."

"I wish, Cam," grinned Angela. "Not so. I need to know how to use numbers to make sure I have enough money in the bank to cover that check to buy the bed. If I don't, I can't write the check, so you don't get a bed."

"Do you see that the purpose for math in this case is to allow me to keep track of how much money we have in the bank? Otherwise, I would spend all of our money on clothing for myself and have nothing left over for your allowance. Does that sound like a good reason for using math?"

"You bet!" exclaimed Cameron.

"Another thing. You wanted to buy a new CD player. There was one advertised at 30% off the regular price. Remember I showed you how to figure that out so you'd know if you had enough money in the bank to pay for it?"

"Yeah. I forgot about that. Wow! I never thought math was that kind of stuff. I thought it was only boring school stuff that would never help me."

"Anything can seem useless if you don't understand its purpose. But once you do, suddenly, it makes sense. It has value to you. When you know how to organize numbers and put them in the right order to get the answers you need, math won't be such a bothersome subject for you. You might even learn to like it."

" Well," said Cam hesitantly. "Maybe. At least I'll know how to figure out what you owe me for allowance!"

Angela grinned. "Let's take a look at that test!"

Pro-Active Reflection

CHAPTER

5

Down to the Basics

"Cameron's Teachable Moment"

*I*sn't it interesting how a thought-provoking story like Cameron's can make us think about life's situations in a different light?

I'm sure we could all empathize with the frustration that Cameron felt over the result of his Math test. When he tried to justify himself, many of us may even have smiled as we recalled situations when we've done the same thing. Justifying provides a temporary escape from reality, just as it did for Cameron. It's an easy trap to fall into, isn't it?

The big problem is that many people carry on this justification process for years, often not realizing the effect it has on their lives.

You may even be able to think of someone you know who has never learned to *face the music* as Cameron did with the help of his mother. These people miss out on the teachable moments of life and rob themselves of growth opportunities.

Even though we may not always be happy about it, life delivers many of these learning moments. The most interesting part is that they seem to be uniquely tailored for each and every one of us. Often, we don't even notice them, much less learn from them; we just continue to plod along, wondering why we don't pass the *tests of life*. Ironic, isn't it?

The sad reality is that many don't know how to recognize these moments or learn from them. Part of the problem is a lack of awareness of a very important key –proactive reflection. Through reflection, one can *experience* these moments by putting oneself into a given situation and *relating* to and *learning* from it, without actually participating in it.

Let's try this process of reflection with Cameron's situation.

Could you relate to him? Have you ever walked through the rain with your boots dragging? Have you looked for the deepest puddles

Rene Says

Organization is the greatest form of responsibility in this life. When you choose to exercise your spirit's will upon the people, objects or thoughts that form your environment, you are taking responsibility for your life. You immediately portray a sense of direction that others recognize and respect. Instantaneously your life improves. Otherwise, you float through life being acted upon like a ship without a rudder – that's not very comforting. As a matter of fact, it's plain frightening. Try running a production plant without a schedule. Better yet, take your scout troop out for a 6-day camp

Continued next page...

to walk in, as most children do? Have you ever felt the utter hopelessness that Cameron felt when he acknowledged that *math had defeated him*? You know, that total feeling of disgust in the pit of your stomach when you know you've really blown it – a time when your self-esteem has taken a major beating? Have you sometimes felt paralyzed by your feelings of defeat, as Cameron did?

Many of you could also relate to Angela as she took one look at Cameron's face and instantly recognized his need for a mentor, not a lecture.

Challenging, isn't it – trying to facilitate learning for someone else? It's especially difficult when the learner won't allow humility to replace stubbornness.

We've all taken turns being *the Cameron* of the story at some point in our lives. While some of us learned and moved forward as he did, others continue to blame *the math teacher* for the failing grade on *the test of life.*

Fortunately, Cameron was not left alone to try to solve his problem; he had help in the form of an experienced sage mentor – his mother, Angela. She knew how to effectively use *FaithSkills* with their associated Essential Foundations to help Cameron learn how to satisfy his *inward* needs for *acceptance* and *knowledge.*

Angela chose the common and familiar element of water to facilitate the learning process. Why? Because water illustrates many of the all-encompassing basics of the *fundamental* foundations that Cameron needed to learn about to be successful in math.

Let us consider **Organization** the first of the fundamental foundations.

All things in this world, including you, are *organized* in some fashion. Water is no exception. If it is not organized, it will carve out its own path without regard for anyone or anything else, often wreaking havoc in Nature. Think of the damage caused by flooding – water *unorganized*, if you will. When it is organized, however, such as for use in dams that generate hydro-electric power, or reservoirs used for irrigation, it serves useful purposes.

Sages understand that the same applies in life. Without organization to control our direction, we become distracted and frustrated, unable to achieve our desired goals. Just as Cameron realized that water must be organized in order to be useful, we, too, must organize ourselves and the elements in our lives to accomplish our

Rene Says

without an itinerary. I'll guarantee you a breakdown if you don't organize the events. Notice how organized individuals always seem to radiate a sense of purpose. Doesn't that give you a sense of self worth? No wonder organizers are often propelled into positions of leadership. Have you ever noticed people's reactions when they realize they don't have to do the organizing because you've already done it? It's great, isn't it? OK – besides your mother-in-law who has everything already organized. There is comfort when there's organization – it's critical to our very existence..

purposes.

When we do this, we are satisfying the first of our *fundamental needs*, that of acceptance. We need to feel that we belong, so we organize ourselves and our circumstances accordingly. We try to spend most of our time with people that like us and accept us for who we are. We attend events where we feel comfortable and try to avoid those that threaten our sense of belonging. We often arrange to go to social events with friends, rather than go alone, so we know that we can rely on at least one group to accept us. At the extreme end of this longing, we may even be willing to sacrifice our freedoms, integrity, health, and dreams to try to ensure our acceptance by someone else.

Reflect for a moment on your life. Do you feel accepted within your circles of influence? If not, why not? What do you do to try to facilitate it? Have you sometimes *organized* people or events in your life according to the patterns as previously mentioned? When you do feel accepted, does this change the way you *organize* yourself and the people or circumstances in your life? Why?

Sage individuals understand that they must take action and *organize* essential parts of their lives if they expect to meet their desired goals. They fully recognize that they can't expect results without effort.

Sages also realize that everything existing in this world is the result of a pattern of organization. They know that since matter cannot be destroyed, its opposite must also be true – matter cannot mysteriously appear; it's simply organized or re-organized into the state in which we see or experience it. This principle explains why Sages have the following attitude:

"There's nothing new under the sun."

Do you now recognize the role that organization plays in satisfying your need for acceptance? When you use this knowledge in your own life's circumstances, how could the results be different from those you've known before? How could the sage attitude have an influence in your life?

Go ahead, take the time to write your thoughts down in the adjoining boxes we've provided.

Did you consider these benefits?

• You know that everything that exists in this world is formed according to some pattern. When you analyze and determine what that pattern is, there are no more mysteries, only discoveries that can enhance your quality of life.

• Once you discover the relevant patterns applicable in your circumstances – whether they involve following particular methods for finishing renovations on your house, or arranging a training conference for your employees – you will no longer feel intimidated or powerless because you will now have control over the situation.

Focus Box

My thoughts...

Organization suggests **Order**
the second of the *fundamental foundations*.

Consider this thought. When there's been confusion in your life, did you feel a sense of order? On the other hand, when you've enjoyed harmony, did you recognize an order? This understanding emphasizes the truth of the related sage attitude:

"There's an order to all things."

Cameron was also reminded of this truth when he and Angela discussed cooking macaroni. It could not have been cooked first and the water added later – the water had to go into the pot first.

Many routines in our lives are completed according to an order, but we probably don't even think about it – things like morning rituals, dishes, running errands, and so on. Order usually makes our necessary tasks easier and faster to complete.

This foundation of order helps to satisfy our *fundamental need* for **acceptance**.

Angela knew that as she directed the conversation to present information to Cameron in an orderly way, logically moving from one idea to another, he would be able to make sense out of his situation and find his own successful solutions to his problems. The result? He felt useful and thus, acceptable – his self-esteem was restored.

Is it empowering to know that there is an order to all things – that there really is nothing you can't understand if you discover its order? How could this foundation and its associated attitude have empowered you in the past when you were making a difficult decision? Don't hesitate. Be spontaneous. Jot down your thoughts in the box to the right.

Order is often recognized in the form of patterns. Can you see the tremendous benefits you can derive from creating your own patterns, such as working out daily, changing your eating habits, or choosing an employee of the month? Do you now recognize how this ability to form patterns can empower you to form the new habits you want and dismantle the ones that hold you back?

This brings us to **Purpose**
the third of the *fundamental foundations.*

As expressed in the sage attitude,

"There's an answer for every why."

Many of you may wonder about this statement, as you recall the frustration and confusion you've felt in the past when you've asked the question *why* and concluded that there was no answer to your problem. You felt unsettled because your *fundamental need* for **knowledge**, or answers, was not satisfied.

Cameron felt the same. He saw no answer to the question, "Why do I need math?" However, Angela knew that by helping him understand the foundations

Focus Box

My thoughts...

Focus Box

My thoughts...

of organization and order, he could discover the answers for himself by drawing on knowledge he already had, but didn't recognize.

Likewise, you too are now aware of these same foundations and can use them to answer the *whys* in your life. Reflect on the examples we have thus far provided, as you begin to organize elements, events, or people in a relevant order The reasons for things will become more apparent and you will find solutions that have previously eluded you.

You will also be able to avoid the trap of self-pity as you consciously implement an attitude of "Why is this happening?" and "What am I supposed to learn from this?" rather than blaming someone or something else. You'll never allow yourself to be the victim again.

Now let's reflect for a moment. Can you think of examples of past opportunities that were lost because you didn't understand this foundation of purpose? Now that you are aware of it, how could it be of benefit to you in your various *leadership* roles of parent, employer or salesman? Jot down your thoughts in the box to the left.

As you begin to understand, internalize and apply The Essential

Foundations, you will also begin to develop and demonstrate *FaithSkills*. You will recall that we introduced these to you in Chapter One. There are 13 *FaithSkills* talents, each of which is applied through a foundation to satisfy a *fundamental need*. One or more of these will be discussed in association with each story until you have learned about all of them.

Three *FaithSkills* talents will be discussed in connection with Cameron's story. The first of these is Stewardship.

Stewardship is the *FaithSkill* developed through the foundation of organization. It means to take responsibility for something or someone without taking ownership.

Stewarding uses a *we* attitude – one that fosters the common good, not one that satisfies an individual's greed or desire for control. It demonstrates accountability. Sage stewards know that they are responsible for results and will educate themselves about the best ways to achieve them. They will seek to organize situations and/or *players* to promote team-building rather than use controlling or dictatorial approaches to get results.

As a conscientious parent, Angela was aware of her responsibility for successful results with Cameron. She organized a plan that used familiar examples and directed questioning to guide him in understanding principles that he already knew about but didn't know how to use. Once he understood, he could use them to not only figure out answers to his current questions but to future ones as well. He now had an enhanced problem-solving ability.

Reflect for a moment. Think of a time when you were entrusted with stewardship over someone else's property, child, and/or authority.

Did you accomplish what you needed to with that stewardship? Why or why not? Now that you have an enhanced understanding of the principles of stewarding, would the results have been different if

Focus Box

My thoughts...

you had used these in your past situation? Use the box to the left to express your thoughts.

Angela also taught Cameron about the second *FaithSkill*, **Obedience**. It is related to the foundation of order.

For Cameron to be successful in math, he had to know, understand and obey the laws and patterns of order that govern numbers.

People who are sage know from experience that obedience to the *rules* that govern success is critical if they are to achieve their desired goals, thus, by self-motivated study and analysis, they gain knowledge about what these *rules* are, how they relate to success and the order in which they must be applied to achieve desired results.

Do you now see the need to discover and understand the rules that govern the successes you desire?

The third *FaithSkill* is **Devotion**, which relates to the foundation of purpose.

Once Sages clearly understand the reasons why things are as they are, they can then determine what needs to be done to accomplish their goals. They become devoted to their causes and will do what has to be done to bring about a successful conclusion. They know that it can happen because they have effectively organized elements and circumstances, in the proper order, to achieve their purposes.

Angela was sage about these principles. She knew exactly what she was trying to accomplish with Cameron and was devoted to guiding him to discover for himself how he could be successful not only with math, but also with other situations that would arise in the future. She used familiar concepts that he could relate to and continued her *lesson* until he felt confident in his own abilities. Her devotion to her *cause* was evident through her actions.

Have you ever been devoted to a particular cause? What brought about this devotion? Now that you have discovered the foundations of organization, order and purpose, did they play a part in the development of that devotion?

Now, at this point, you may be thinking – "this all sounds good, but it's way beyond me." Remember, this is an ongoing, life-long process – only you can determine how you will proceed, at what pace, and how you will measure your progress. But it can be done – one step at a time!

As you consistently work on implementing the foundations and their related skills, you will become a better person. Other people will begin to see you in a different light because your leadership skills will become more evident. And, you will also see yourself in a different light.

The reason for this is that *FaithSkills* do not stand in isolation. They not only exemplify Essential Foundations, they also develop *virtues*. There are 7 of these in total and they too are related to *FaithSkills*, Essential Foundations and *fundamental needs*. Each story will introduce you to one or more of these virtues. Let's now explain how they can be applied in real-life situations. Since your definition of virtues may be slightly different than ours, please consider the following.

Virtues often start out as individual characteristics.

A characteristic is innate, and is usually for the benefit of the

Ponder This

Supervisors

Isn't it interesting that regardless of the type of supervisor you are – a Mother at home or a plant supervisor – you are automatically expected to keep order and organize anyone and everything in sight to achieve the purposes at hand?

Won't it be easier to guide people now that you understand the interrelationship that organization, order and purpose have to each other?

That's Team Building!

one who possesses it. A behavior is the display of the characteristic for all to see, and if positive, a benefit to those who witness it.

A virtue, however, is an act upon someone else's spirit from the originating spirit – it is action on a spiritual plane. Virtues touch people to the core. They not only witness the action, they feel it.

Virtues are frequently spoken of as *spirits*, because of their influence upon people. We've all heard them mentioned in such common statements as, "he has the true spirit of charity, or, her sincere acts of kindness are felt by all of us."

Virtuous people have touched us all, whether it be the champion who never flaunts his ability, or the handicapped musician that strums the chords of our hearts because of the immense discipline he's applied to learning his instrument in order to present a flawless performance. Actions such as these have touched our spirits and inspired us from within.

Let's consider the virtues that relate to the three Essential Foundations we've already discussed.

Discernment is the *virtue* that relates to the foundations of organization and order.

Sages are effective decision makers because they have learned, through practice, how to separate the important from the unimportant. They carefully consider a given situation to determine which things need to be organized and how, as well as what order would give the best results. They plan with the *end in mind*, so that nothing is left to chance.

Angela used this ability to discern as soon as Cameron walked into the kitchen. She knew immediately that he didn't need to hear a lecture about slamming doors. As he poured out his frustrations, she listened carefully, then mentally formed a *plan of attack.* She used examples that were familiar to him and questions that would direct his attention in ways he hadn't previously considered. Angela was a great example of a discerning parent.

Food for thought. Are you a discerning individual? Could it positively influence your decision-making abilities? Now that you have enhanced your knowledge with this virtue and how it can be formed, could it enhance your self-esteem?

The third foundation discussed here was purpose. Its related *virtue* is **Self-reliance.**

Sages are confident individuals who rely on themselves. They recognize that they have the keys for opening the doors leading to enduring successes – namely, their knowledge of the Essential Foundations and related *FaithSkills.* By faithfully implementing these, they know that they will not only satisfy their *fundamental needs*, but also develop virtues that will enhance their abilities to achieve their goals. Thus, they are independent, not reliant on something or someone else to determine their life's direction.

Angela wanted Cameron to have the same keys, so she didn't

> ### Ponder This
>
> *Managers*
>
> You now know the skills and the virtues they create which can effectively and profoundly influence all those with whom you are entrusted. You are now able to exercise stewardship over your team members, and have them desire to follow your leadership, because your actions will fulfill their individual *fundamental need* for acceptance.
>
> *That's how solid teams are built!*

just give him the answers to his problems. She helped him to recognize a *method* that he could use to solve not only his current problem, but future ones as well. He could then have confidence that he was armed with the tools he needed to help himself in any given situation.

Do you recognize the comfort you feel when you consider the advantages of being self-reliant? Interesting isn't it? It's a powerful virtue that influences people when they witness it. Effectively apply these *FaithSkills* to these new understandings, and you too will develop these life changing virtues.

We hope that our discussion of this story has given you cause for reflection upon your present life and made you say to yourself, "I didn't think of it like that"?

As you do, you will start to discover and recognize the immense capacity you have to succeed and you'll never underestimate your potential again!

Pro-Active Reflection

CHAPTER

6

Opposition

*V*acation. The months had crawled by, but finally the big day had arrived. Relief! Freedom! thought Cindy Harris. I'm going to enjoy every minute of this holiday. She wearily sank down into the luxurious first class seat beside her husband James.

"I can't believe we've waited five years for this holiday!" exclaimed James. "What were we thinking? We should have done this before now!"

"You can say that again!" said Cindy. "Finally. No classes. No parent-teacher interviews. No report cards. I can hardly wait!"

"You said it, honey! The office will probably have a hard time getting along without my sales for the next two weeks, but, too bad! That's their problem. I'm not going to give them, or their electronics equipment, one single thought while we're away. I'm going to forget about everything, and relax, relax, relax!" said James.

Hours later, as they emerged from the airport, he was already drenched in sweat.

"I can't believe this humidity!" said James. "It's a killer!"

"Yes, but look at the gorgeous scenery, James, and smell that air. I'm going to love Cancun," said Cindy excitedly.

James rolled his eyes and reminded himself that the welcome feel of air conditioning was only a taxi away.

After settling themselves in the hotel, he suggested they have a few drinks and then wander down to the beach area.

"Great idea!" said Cindy. "I'm dying to know if everything I've heard about the sand and the blue water is true!"

"Better watch out for sharks!" said James, raising his right eyebrow in the perfect arch he always did when he teased Cindy.

Several drinks later, James was not the least bit worried about the humidity. This is the life, he thought. For the next two weeks, I can let go – have a break from my usual, hard-working, top-producing self. Gone are the suits, ties and social drinks. I'm going to really let loose and put aside my leadership demands. Look out, Cancun – here I come!

Cindy interrupted his thoughts. "Race you to the beach!" she yelled. In a flash, James was out of his seat and through the door.

Beautiful, white sand and blue skies stretched for miles. Blazing sun warmed their backs.

"Can you believe this, Cindy?" asked James.

"Everything I heard about the skies and water is true! Boy, does this beat rainy, cold, dreary Seattle! Maybe we won't want to go home!" yelled Cindy.

As they strolled along the beach, the heat from the sun intensified. Maybe I should have brought a hat, thought James, or at least, some sunscreen, but I didn't feel like going all the way back to the hotel room before we left the lounge. Oh, well, no big deal.

"Hey, James, look at that bazaar over there! Would you mind if I went to look around?" asked Cindy.

"Go ahead, take your time," said James. "I'll just sit here and watch the boats for awhile." He welcomed the chance to sit down. His head was aching. He was feeling a bit woozy. He thought he might be sick. Must be too much sun, he thought. I'm not used to this kind of heat. I'll be OK. Just need to rest a bit.

He eased his exhausted body down onto a blanket just a few feet in front of him. Hope the owner won't mind, he thought. The boats in the distance soon faded from view as his body relaxed and his eyes closed.

An hour later, Cindy returned, her arms overflowing with bargains for friends and family back home. She couldn't believe that she'd actually been gone that long; she would never have taken that kind of time at home! Her eyes twinkled as she thought about what she'd spent – right on budget! She gave herself a pat on the back. Good job, girl!

She could hardly wait to show James her bargains. I'll just sneak up beside him and whisper in his ear – that'll make him jump, she thought.

She slowly snuck up beside him, then froze instantly. Her packages fell in a heap on the sand.

Could this blazing-red, blistered body belong to her husband? Did he move and this was someone else? No, it was James – she'd know that watch anywhere.

"James! James! Wake up!" yelled Cindy.

He slowly opened his eyes. His blank look scared her. He tried to sit up but fell immediately back onto the sand.

"James, it's Cindy. What on earth happened?"

"Cindy? I don't feel very well. Everything hurts."

"I'm not surprised. You've got a terrible sunburn. We need to get you to a hospital!"

In emergency, several doctors hovered over James. If they even breathed on his skin, he screamed in pain. One of the doctors turned to Cindy.

"He has a terrible burn, Mrs. Harris. We see this all the time. People come here to enjoy the sun and don't realize the damage it can do, even in a short period of time. We'll keep your husband here for the next few days so we can make sure there are no complications. We'll also try to make him comfortable."

When Cindy finally got to see him, James was in quite a state. The pain from the burn was intense; so was his level of anger with himself.

"How could I be so stupid, Cindy? What was going on in my head?"

"James, what exactly happened?"

"When you went off to shop, I sat down on the sand intending to watch the boats. I was kind of tired so I thought I'd lay back and close my eyes for just a few minutes."

"So you were laying in that sun for the whole time I was gone?"

"I guess so – I don't exactly remember," said James. He winced in pain as Cindy reached over to lovingly caress his arm.

She felt bad to see him in so much pain and yet.....

"James," said Cindy slowly, "how many drinks did you have before we left the lounge?"

"I don't know. I don't remember."

"Oh......."

"OK, OK, Cindy. I know what you're going to say. If I hadn't had so much to drink, I wouldn't have fallen asleep and I wouldn't be in this mess! But we're on holidays – I just wanted to enjoy myself," exclaimed James.

"Is this what you call enjoyment?" asked Cindy hesitantly.

"No! Do you think I like lying here?" asked James indignantly.

"You know, James, this is an interesting turn of events. We came here because we wanted sun. I...."

James interrupted. "Exactly. We were sick of the rain in Seattle."

"But," said Cindy, "instead of enjoying the sun, we......"

"Yeah, yeah," muttered James. "I'm stuck in a hospital – so much for sun. Maybe if I'd gone back for hats and sunscreen...." His voice trailed off.

"Or," said Cindy quietly, "maybe if we'd left the lounge earlier?"

James glared at her.

It's going to be a long week, thought Cindy.

As she left the hospital, she began to reflect on the situation. Twelve years of married life. In gentle ways, I've tried to help him learn to balance things in his life. Sometimes he does OK with it, and sometimes he doesn't. Holidays are one of those times when he doesn't. But I know that he knows better. What happens to his good sense? Why does his attitude change? How can I help him? One of these days, he's going to get himself into a really difficult situation. I hope we can sort this out before that happens.

Surprisingly, the time passed quickly. By the end of the week,

James was much improved. As Cindy picked him up from the hospital, she told him she'd arranged a surprise.

"Really?" asked James sarcastically. "Would that be an early flight home? I'm not much fun."

"Now, James," said Cindy firmly, "that wouldn't accomplish anything."

"Well, so far, I haven't accomplished much either, except being a nuisance to you."

Cindy ignored his comment, hoping that her surprise would lift his spirits.

"You know how we've often watched the sailboats from our kitchen window at home? We've talked about trying sailing sometime, but never have. Before, we didn't have the time, or the money, but now we do. So, I arranged for us to go this afternoon, James. I thought it would be fun. I hope you're up to it."

"I guess so, as long as I can just sit – and be out of the sun!"

"It might be tricky to avoid the sun, James, but I brought lots of sunscreen for you as well as a light jacket and pants. Ken, our guide, said he would also try to rig up some kind of shelter for you."

True to his word, Ken did exactly as he had promised.

Nice guy, thought James. I hope this all works out – Cindy's gone to a lot of trouble to arrange the trip.

Ken was a real talker. To James and Cindy, it appeared that he was willing to share his entire life history, complete with all the details.

After an hour of sharing his tales, he suddenly paused, and turned his attention to his guests.

"There isn't much I don't know about sailing," he stated matter-of-factly. "How 'bout you two?"

"We've never done it before," explained James, "but we've always wanted to. You see, we live in Seattle. We see sailboats all the time, and have often wondered what it was like to be on one. It must be fun – there sure are a lot of people doing it."

Ken nodded. "It's a great pastime – kind of gets in your blood."

"What's so appealing about it?" inquired James.

Ken answered without even thinking. "It's the freedom. I can sail out on the ocean for as long and as far as I want to. I sit back and enjoy the blue skies, the lap of the waves against the boat, and the wind."

"The wind?" asked Cindy.

"For sure," said Ken. "That's the whole secret to sailing a boat – knowing how to control what can kill you!"

"Kill you?" questioned Cindy. She shuddered as she stole a glance at James. He wasn't looking too well.

"Yep," said Ken emphatically. "If you don't control it, it's the enemy – can send you crashing into everything you don't want to be close to. But if you know how to use it, you can go around the whole world and see stuff you never thought you'd lay your eyes on."

"Sounds like a pretty delicate balancing act," said James.

"It is. You don't need too many hair-raising experiences to help you figure out that you want the wind on your side."

"So you're saying that you need the opposition of the wind to make the boat go where you want it to, but you always need to know how to balance that opposition so you can avoid disaster," explained James.

"Exactly," said Ken. "They've got to be in perfect harmony, one with the other, in order for you to get the most out of the wind."

Wow, thought Cindy. Maybe James is beginning to get the idea. Balance helps avoid disaster – he said it himself. This little trip is going to help us far more than I ever thought it would. I think the teachable moment has finally come, and I didn't even have to set the stage – Ken did that for me. Where did he go? Looks like he's busy at the back of the boat. He won't be able to hear us. Perfect. This is it!

"How's the trip so far, James?" asked Cindy.

"Great. I'm really enjoying it. Ken's pretty interesting. That stuff he said about balance and opposition – I hadn't thought about it like that before. Did you?"

Cindy tried to control the huge smile that was about to break over her face.

"Well, actually, I have been thinking about those very things, James. That whole idea applies very well to you and me."

"It does? What do you mean?"

"We're very different people in many ways – kind of like opposing forces. I tend to be in control and focused most of the time, while you sometimes go to extremes. I'm one who likes to be alone, but you enjoy being with people. How do we manage these differences, James?"

He thought for a moment. "Well, we encourage each other so we can usually avoid having too much of one thing and not enough of something else. I guess that's ......balance?"

"Absolutely!" said Cindy excitedly. "By doing this, we can direct things in ways that will help us both to meet our goals, not destroy them. Now think about this holiday. Has balance played a role here?"

James looked sheepish. He waited for a long time before answering. "Not exactly," he said slowly. "My excuse was that I was on holidays, so I should be able to do what I wanted. I went to the extreme again, and look what happened – the disaster that Ken said would happen, happened, because I didn't have control of myself. Wrong attitude again! I hate to think of the number of times this kind of thing has happened. Boy, am I a slow learner!"

Cindy wanted to jump up and hug him. Pay dirt, she thought.

"But, James, the fact that you recognize the problem is the beginning to amazing progress. Like Ken said, opposition – the wind – is needed to make the boat move, just like it's needed to help us achieve our goals. If everything always went smoothly, we would never have a reason to stretch, so we wouldn't improve ourselves. And without balance, we'd live lives of extremes, which wouldn't accomplish what we want either."

"Well," said James thoughtfully, "I guess we've learned something today. Who would have thought that the teacher would be a middle-aged, crusty old sailor?"

"Thanks to that crusty old sailor, this has turned out to be the best holiday we've ever had," exclaimed Cindy.

"Absolutely!" agreed James. "But let's not wait 5 years for the next one!"

Pro-Active Reflection

CHAPTER 7

It's Black and White

"James's Teachable Moment"

*L*ife provides interesting challenges, doesn't it? They take many different forms and come in many different circumstances. The trick in dealing with them successfully is perspective.

In this story, we've hopefully presented a different perspective for you to consider – one that will make a difference in your progress towards greater successes in your life.

Those of you who are reading this story want to achieve greater success in your lives, or you wouldn't have purchased this book. You're more than likely what we here at The Sage Academy refer to as new entrepreneurs. No matter what happens, you're the ones responsible for results. Others often count on your actions to determine their day, so you could relate to James and his wife, Cindy. They were both responsible people. They got things done. Both assumed leadership roles in their own fields. However, James wasn't a balanced individual; he was in a rut. His tendency to live by extremes was hampering his growth, and sadly, he wasn't fully aware of it.

Many of us have experienced this at one time or another. Often it takes a *deer-in-the-headlights* experience – something that brings us up short – to help us refocus and get back on track. For James, his *deer* experience was a painful sunburn that he brought upon himself by his own actions. It humbled him to a point where a gentle mentor – his wife, Cindy – could teach him.

You see, Cindy was sage about this issue. She had learned from the experiences of others, as well as her own, that it's important in life to recognize the foundations of balance and opposition and the part they play in reaching goals. Once understood, assimilated and applied, they can help individuals achieve harmony, and in turn, greater successes.

It was these sage understandings that empowered Cindy to use her *FaithSkills* to help James understand the foundations for himself, permanently, by offering an example to which he could totally relate – themselves.

Let us consider **Balance**
the first of the *leveling foundations*.

Balance is an integral part of life. Consider the relationship between James and Cindy. They had different interests and ways of doing things. If left to themselves, both would tend to their natural extremes and possibly never know the benefits of the other's approach. With encouragement, however, each could participate in the opposite experience and appreciate it for what it offered. These actions helped to satisfy their innate *fundamental need* for **harmony**.

Sage individuals recognize that maintaining balance helps to avoid extremes that interfere with the spirit's complete fulfillment.

Ponder this thought for a moment.

Have you as a developing sage individual been aware of times when you needed balance within yourself – you know, for whatever reason you just knew you were experiencing too much of a good thing, or worse, too much of a bad thing?

Now that you've read the chapter about *fundamental needs*, you know that the *force* of your spirit's *fundamental need* for comfort is more than physical. If misunderstood, however, it will usually drive you to physical extremes that often provide immediate, but short-lived, levels of comfort.

James found this to be true. He pounced on the opportunity to enjoy physical comfort, thinking that it would provide well-deserved fun and relaxation – the opposite of the office drudgery he had escaped – but he went too far.

Have you had similar experiences where you've overdone

something, and then you yourself suffered the uncomfortable consequences of being "*overdone*" as James did? What could you have done to bring balance to the situation?

Sages have adopted the attitude that is built upon the foundation of balance:

"You Need Balance to Have Harmony."

Carefully reflect for a moment. How can your newly enhanced understanding of balance clarify your own choices, as well as influence the results of your interactions with other people and circumstances?

Now that you understand the *fundamental need* for harmony or comfort that often drives us to points of extreme or imbalance, will you look at your own actions more carefully from an inner point of view to make sure that they truly do satisfy your innate need for harmony?

As you reflect, you may be asking yourself questions that you never thought would influence your decisions – such questions as: Do alcohol, drugs or tobacco really bring me true comfort? Have I misinterpreted physical comfort for the harmony that my spirit needs?

Focus Box

My thoughts...

85

Think about it

Esteem is an action word – it requires effort. Unless you apply yourself, you'll never be able to esteem yourself as your spirit knows you should. So, get on with it. Esteem yourself so you can become what you are meant to be!

Will a better paying job give me more money to pay the bills but demand more working hours and actually give my family harmony? Sure the physical needs and even wants will be taken care of, but will it balance my family's quality of life? Will more energy, thus stress, be created trying to spend time with your family?

Achieving and maintaining balance in life is an ongoing, lifelong learning process. We must consider this process in everything we do – whether it be eating, making money, playing, reading, loving, canning food, and so on. If we don't, we may find ourselves going to extremes and complicating our lives even further.

Let us now consider **Opposition**
the second of the *leveling foundations*.

This foundation also helps to satisfy our *fundamental need* for harmony, or comfort.

Whenever balance is required, opposition will be present. This is a given, but not necessarily a negative one.

Consider these examples. In order to truly understand what *light* is, we need exposure to *dark*. To fully appreciate what *health* is, we need to experience *illness*. To deeply understand *happiness*, we have to know *sorrow*.

Remember, *experiencing* does not necessarily mean *doing*. For example, you don't have to do drugs to know they're bad. Ask anyone who's lost a loved one to them!

James and Cindy had learned something about opposition

during their years of marriage, as most couples have. As Cindy reminded James, they were very different people, with different attitudes, personalities and ways of doing things. However, through a continual process of *give and take*, they learned to use these differences constructively.

Do you now feel empowered to face opposition with a desire to use it to your advantage, rather than fight it?

Sage individuals understand that challenges help us to define ourselves – to know what we're really made of. Facing them and conquering them not only gives us courage, but also belief in ourselves that we can deal with the new ones that will always present themselves!

They also know from experience that there is a profound truism expressed in the sage attitude that:

"You Need to Know Bad
to Know Good."

Can you appreciate why opposition is a necessary part of life? Does this change your attitude towards it? If you had had your current understanding of opposition in past experiences, would it have changed the

Focus Box

My thoughts...

87

results of the situation?

As you will recall from the story, Ken's sharing of his sailing experiences also helped James gain a new perspective about opposition.

Ken had learned how to use the wind as an ally. By obeying its *rules*, he used it to achieve his goal of moving the boat where he wanted it to go. He couldn't make the wind blow when he wanted it to nor could he change its speed when it did blow. His choice was to make adjustments with the boat.

His sage attitude to opposition made a major difference in his approach to sailing. He understood that if he recognized it, then devised tactics to make it work to his advantage, it wouldn't destroy or cripple him, but empower him to reach destinations he could only dream of.

You have likely had many experiences with opposition. So have Sages. They realize that sometimes we bring it on ourselves, and other times, it comes from outside sources. Regardless, they realize, as you do, that everyone must decide what they're going to do with it.

As one who is responsible for results, you've learned that if you don't face it and deal with it appropriately, a myriad of other problems can result.

You've likely also learned from experience that challenges bring growth that might not come in any other way.

An understanding of these two *leveling* foundations of balance and opposition prepares one to develop the associated *FaithSkills* of Cooperation and Fearlessness.

Cooperation is an essential skill that relates to balance. Effective Sages *"steward"* – they're not dictators, but rather, facilitators. They coach others to cooperate without destroying their self-esteem.

Cindy knew that her discussions with James could have been very unpleasant, but she had faith in herself that she could direct them in such a way that James would be encouraged to cooperate, not retaliate.

She helped him to learn from his sunburn experience by asking him questions that directed his thoughts inward so he could realize for himself that changes needed to be made.

I'm sure that at some point in time you've witnessed solid cooperation in action. How did it affect the people involved or the results of the activity?

With the perfect vision of hindsight that reflection offers, do you yourself, as a leader in a project, fail to use the skill of cooperation? Do you now see that you may have to change some of your ideas, or maybe let go of them altogether, in order to encourage cooperation from your team members? As the facilitator, how do you feel about the process? Don't rush. Take the time to record your thoughts in the box to the right.

Fearlessness is the second *FaithSkill*. It is related to the foundation of opposition.

Sages have learned that fearlessness often requires putting their own feelings or fears aside for the sake of preserving relationships or taking advantage of opportunities as they present themselves.

Focus Box

My thoughts...

Focus Box

My thoughts...

Ken was an excellent example of this. His sailing experiences had taught him a great deal about taking advantage of opportunities.

He'd learned that when the wind – the opposition – blew, he had to have the sails up and ready to *"cooperate"* with that driving force. If he'd put them in place only when he felt comfortable, or according to patterns that he wanted to use regardless of what was necessary, he couldn't have harnessed the power of the wind to achieve his purposes.

As he said, "You could get killed," but that didn't stop him from facing his skills directly into the winds of opposition to gain the freedom that sailing offered.

Cindy also exhibited her *FaithSkill* of fearlessness, but in quite a different way. When the sailing trip offered the long-awaited teachable moment, she recognized her opportunity and steered the conversation accordingly.

If she had been selfish and more concerned about James suffering the consequences of his actions, she would have left him back at the hotel to stew on the consequences of his actions. He likely would have continued living the life of imbalance he'd repeated so many times before. Instead she demonstrated courage and brought the issue to a creative and constructive head - without any lecture, Cindy delivered the teachable moment to James in a way that empowered him. In fact the circumstances could have easily disabled and damaged him. This could have had disastrous results for their marriage.

List some situations in your life that you may now realize the skill of fearlessness could have been applied to. How would the results have been different if it had been? Would those situations have been more positive?

Thus far, we have discussed the *FaithSkills* of Cooperation and Fearlessness. You have now learned about five of the thirteen *FaithSkills*, the other three being Stewardship, Obedience and Devotion.

These *FaithSkills* are so named because they facilitate the empowerment of your spirit upon your body, and thus your life, which is a manifestation of the practical skill called faith. With faith, your spiritual confidence can act upon your life rather than have your life act upon you.

As you already know, work on strengthening your *FaithSkills*, and you'll develop virtues.

Patience is the *virtue* that results from effective implementation of the foundations of balance and opposition and their related attitudes.

It is a major key to success. Sages understand that patience fuels discipline – the ability to focus one's efforts in any and all aspects of life, regardless of other distractions. It drives an individual to

> ## Think about it
>
> A virtue is a characteristic that touches the spirits of others. That's why it is often referred to as a *spirit*, such as in the saying, *he's got the true spirit of charity*. The powerful influence of a virtue can often move others to actually improve themselves.

Ponder This

Husbands and Wives
Do you see how positive the results can be when both of you exercise faith in yourselves, and in each other with *FaithSkills*? You can teach and guide one another when there are difficulties to overcome.
Why is it sometimes hard to do? Probably because you're too busy taking care of your temporal needs rather than satisfying your fundamental needs – your spirit's needs. Trust one another again like you did on your wedding day, the day where you exercised ultimate faith in one another.

not only set worthwhile goals, but to put in his or her best efforts to accomplish them.

In our story, both Cindy and James exercised patience. Cindy was quite aware that at some point in time, a teachable moment would arise so she could help her husband improve his ability to achieve balance in his life. She didn't know when this would occur, but was always prepared for when it did happen.

James too had developed the virtue of patience in his business. He was one of the top producers in his company – an accomplishment that wouldn't have happened without disciplined goal setting and patient, sustained effort.

Patience suggests obedience. Sages have learned that patient obedience to *governing laws*, both written and unwritten, more often than not yields positive, not negative results. Obedience requires patience, especially if the validity of the *law* seems questionable.

Ken knew this to be true. He had respect for the workings of both the wind and the water, knowing that without proper use of the wind and the boat, the water could destroy him – a harsh, but unavoidable consequence.

As one who is striving to improve yourself, you must be familiar with the results when you exercise patience with yourself and with life's circumstances. You also know very well what happens when you don't. The key is to build upon these new

92

understandings to make the permanent positive changes you want in your life. They're inevitable when you create your own life of permanent success.

Isn't it empowering to know that you can incorporate an understanding of balance and opposition into your life and make both of them work to your advantage?

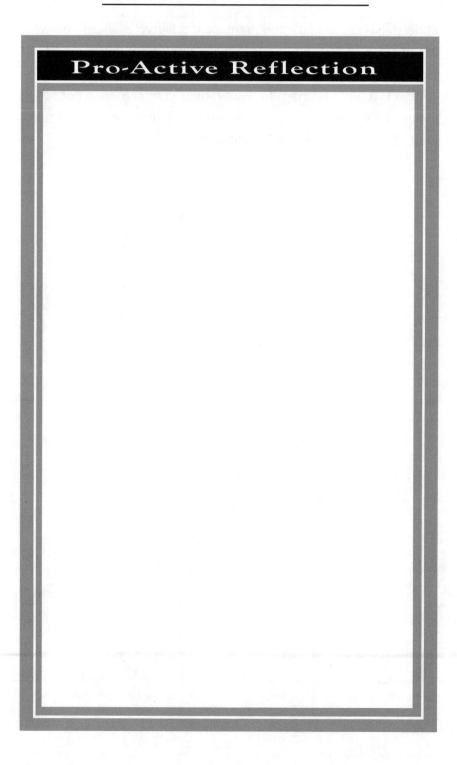

Pro-Active Reflection

CHAPTER

8

Sage Reflections

"How do you know where you're going
if you don't know where you're at?"

*T*hat's a question a wise old man once asked me when we were doing some strategic planning. You see, you need to know your bearings – where you are right now – before you can plan your next step. That's the purpose of these reflective moments.

Here's an experience from one of our team members that might further explain why we include reflective moments throughout this book.

"My husband knows no fear. Take skiing for instance. He learned on a slope that by most people's standards would be considered an *expert* run – the slope changed to a steeper grade every 10 feet! His friends told him that if he could learn to ski there, he'd be comfortable anywhere. He learned and did a great job!"

"Then there's me. I know fear all too well. My husband wanted to teach me how to ski. He actually expected me to strap my feet onto some slippery, narrow pieces of board and slide down a hill with only 2 skinny pieces of metal to help me stop. Yeah, right! Any hill, no matter how minor the slope, looked to me like a long, long, LONG vertical drop. Then, to top it all off, I looked up the hill and saw one of the attendants on the slope. *He had a hook hand!* I was absolutely convinced that he'd had some terrible accident on the slopes and that the hook was the result. *I was terrified.*

"But, that didn't stop my husband's lesson. He thought it should be easy for me because it had been easy for him. He thought, he was taking me slowly from step 1 to step 2. But to me, he was taking me from step 1 to step 40, in five minutes or less. He couldn't relate to my fear, so he wasn't able to reach me on my level and teach me accordingly."

"Needless to say, that was my first and last skiing experience!"

Many of you may be chuckling to yourself as you remember

similar incidents in your own life. You already know the problem. Our team member and her husband were not at the same beginning point, so effective learning didn't happen.

We don't want that same frustration for you, so our reflective moments are designed to begin where you are – at your present level of understanding – and build from there. We will endeavor to break down the information into *bite-sized* pieces so we take you slowly from one step to the next.

It is our hope that by the end of the reflective moment you will be able to say "Ah-ha! Now it makes sense!" You will then be prepared to understand the information presented in the chapters that follow.

As we begin this reflective moment, some of you probably feel like the husband did in our story – you're confident in your ability to understand, the pace for presenting the information was good, you see that it has a lot of merit, and you want to learn more – Good! Then this reflective moment will provide a solid review for you – you'll be able to effectively deepen your ability to relate to the material.

On the other hand, some of you may feel like the rookie on the slope – too much information coming at you too quickly. If that is the case, this *moment* will break down the information you've read into *bite-sized* pieces so you can *eat at your own pace*.

So, sit back and put your feet up. Remember – take your time. No one is putting pressure on you; your expectations are your own. Let your spirit and your mind *reason* together as we take another look at what you've just read.

The first thing you learned was this: as human beings, we all have deep innate needs that come from our spirit which drive our ambitions. Our needs must be met if we want to be satisfied, or fulfilled, in this life. They are the same for everyone; that's why we call them Our *fundamental needs*.

Consider for a moment how these needs form an important part of your life. You may have recognized some of these in the past, while others have been, or are, masqueraded in the form of money, cars, and other toys of this world.

But now you know what these *currents* really are and how they translate into what drives your ambitions; you also discovered where they come from – your spirit.

Let's briefly review these *currents* and their associated Foundations and *FaithSkills*.

Acceptance is the need to belong. We all want to be accepted for who we really are, whether in our families, amongst our friends, or within our working environments. If it doesn't happen, we either resign ourselves to it and feel unhappy and unfulfilled, or we look for it somewhere else – we will do whatever we can to facilitate some form of acceptance.

Sometimes, we even use our possessions as a drawing card. Although we know deep down that people don't have a genuine interest in us, we still hope that acceptance might evolve from the situation.

We never stop looking for this until our spirit is fully accepted by at least one individual – we're talking about Love!

Do you agree that you have this need? What do you do to satisfy it? Do your methods vary, depending on the people and/or circumstances involved?

Knowledge is the need to have answers to the *whys* in our lives. We, our spirits, really want to understand why we're here, and what we're supposed to be doing.

Have you wondered about this yourself? Maybe you've also wondered why certain things have happened in your life and why they couldn't be different.

Our spirits know that there are answers for everything, so it's perfectly normal to ask the question *why*. They know that we're here to learn all we can about ourselves through this environment, so it's okay to be curious. As you may recall, our spirits know that we possess enormous intelligence, and they want to translate it into knowledge through our bodies. As a matter of fact, that's their job!

Harmony is the need for comfort in life. We're much more content when things are running smoothly. When there's an absence of confusion and contention, we're happy. Would you agree?

Most of us look for ways to bring about this peacefulness – the methods will vary from person to person, or spirit to spirit. Whatever you do, you need to be at peace with yourself or your spirit won't rest until you are.

Think about the last time you had an experience with nature. Was it peaceful? Did you enjoy it?

Do you now know why many of us feel at peace in nature? Because everything connects there. Nothing is out of order. Our spirit recognizes the harmony and comes to rest. It's awesome!

Identity is the need to know who you are. Yes, you know that you're someone's husband or wife, cousin, parent, friend, doctor, etc. but isn't there more to it than that? Our spirit knows that by having a physical body we can discover who we really are.

We have the awesome opportunity of utilizing this precious instrument (the body), to discover our strengths and weaknesses. With the will of our spirits, we can turn our weaknesses into strengths so we can grow in capacity and ability.

This concept of identity may still be a bit foggy. That's okay, as it's likely one of the most mind boggling, yet intriguing ideas you've heard. Chapter 9 will explain it further.

Direction is the need to know how you will accomplish your purposes in life. We are all innately driven towards achieving objectives. That's because our spirits *know* that our purpose here is to use our bodies to discover and increase our capacities. We must have direction in our days, or we get discouraged, even depressed, because our spirits are confused.

Are you happy with the direction you're presently taking? Would you like to improve the leadership skills you use at home or in the office? Do you want to improve your plans in order to achieve more of your goals?

Obviously, you do – that's why you're reading this book. This *current* is acting upon you as you read; it recognizes the validity of what you're discovering.

Empowerment is the need to exercise your will – your ability to choose – upon your environment.

Have you ever been in a situation where your right to choose was taken away from you? Did you feel "trapped" or "powerless"? What did you do, or what were you willing to do, to get it back? Think about World War II. The Korean War. Any war, for that matter. Aren't they all about choice?

If we've never had this privilege removed, maybe we need that experience to appreciate the value of choice. It is the essence of freedom. It is absolute empowerment.

Fulfillment is the need to achieve. Our spirits *know* that just being here is a success. It is fulfillment of a desire or goal that we had before we came here.

Progression is the very essence of our existence. That's why it's perfectly natural to have goals that we want to achieve. When we do, our self-esteem is enhanced – we feel good about ourselves because of the contribution we've been able to make. This is a powerful *current* that affects the way we look at ourselves and everything else that happens to us.

Because our spirits are in unfamiliar territory – this physical world – they often allow our physical dimension to decide how we quench this need for fulfillment. It becomes our default Personal

Operating System, thus, we often misinterpret the accumulation of possessions, or the attention and praise they bring, as fulfillment of the need. Sound familiar? We've all experienced the short-term happiness that the *toys* from this life give us; the problem is, they don't provide enduring fulfillment. As a matter of fact, they often fuel the appetite of *want* which overpowers the nutrition of *need*, and off we go on the roller coaster of frustration.

Have you been in these situations yourself? Do you know people who are? The consequences are often overwhelming, not to mention frightening.

We hope that you noticed that fulfillment is the 7th *fundamental need*. It is the *result* of successfully satisfying the 6 needs that precede it. If one or more of the previous needs have not been satisfied, you will find yourself feeling restless and uncomfortable – in short, unfulfilled.

No matter what your successes are, or have been, they will not be enduring if they aren't built upon satisfying these *fundamental needs* in the order in which they've been presented. You will not be able to sustain any sense of long-term fulfillment because your spirit will be confused and want more.

Now that you've discovered the 7 *fundamental needs* of your spirit, you understand that a spiritually based operating system would be far more effective in meeting these deep and powerful needs than a physically based system.

How are you doing so far? Do you understand the material? Can you relate to the examples we've provided?

This next section of our reflective moment will review the Essential Foundations and *FaithSkills*.

Each of the *fundamental needs* has one or more Essential Foundations through which it must be fulfilled. There are a total of 13 Essential Foundations; they are divided into 6 categories. As you may remember, these Foundations are understandings that act as solid supports upon which to build our skills and talents in order to meet our needs through our daily actions.

In Chapter 4, you learned about the 1st category of these foundations, namely the *fundamental* foundations, which are Organization, Order and Purpose. Organization and Order satisfy our *fundamental need* for acceptance or belonging, while Purpose satisfies our need to know the *whys* of things – in other words, to have knowledge.

In Chapter 6, you discovered the *leveling* foundations of Balance and Opposition, which fall into the second category of Essential Foundations. These satisfy our *fundamental need* for harmony.

To help you make sense of these needs and foundations, we presented 2 parables, or stories, so you could see how they fit into life's experiences. Hopefully, as you read them you could say to yourself, "I've felt that way" or "I see what they're trying to say". This is the process of relating – in other words, understanding how the stories can apply to you.

The parables also used familiar

Focus Box

My thoughts...

103

concepts (water in Chapter 4 and vacation time in Chapter 6) as teaching tools so you could easily relate to them. I hope that as you use the power of reflection, these familiar elements of life help you look at things differently than you did before – to *see through different glasses* so to speak, *spiritual glasses.*

In the summaries of the stories, we introduced you to 5 of the *FaithSkills*, namely, Stewardship, Obedience, Devotion, Cooperation and Fearlessness.

Do you remember how stewards influence learning?

Effective stewards strive to build effective teams, whether at home or in the workplace, so they *coach* rather than *preach* or *dictate.* Their interest is to teach others how to accomplish their goals by starting where those individuals are in their understanding, then building from there until the goals are accomplished. In short, stewards are effective facilitators of learning. They also realize that *the very essence of obedience is the spirit acting upon the body.*

Had you previously considered devotion, cooperation and fearlessness as *spirit-based* skills? How could this view change your feelings about their influence on your life?

Remember that there are 13 *FaithSkills* altogether. Collectively, they fall under the title of *practical faith.* In other words, there are 13 smaller pieces (*FaithSkills*) that form the whole (*practical faith*).

As we develop each skill in our own way, we develop faith. Faith, then, is different for all of us. It is a new and personal talent that only you can develop. As a matter of fact, it's so new and unfamiliar to us, that there is often much confusion surrounding it. Why? Our intelligences don't recognize it, because until now, we never had bodies for our spirits to act upon. We didn't understand that our *fundamental needs* come from our spirits and can only be satisfied by our spirits. (Chapter Nine will explain this concept further.)

Practical faith not only allows, but also empowers our spirits to act upon our lives to satisfy these needs and help us feel joy.

Hopefully, you've already recognized that The Essential Foundations and *FaithSkills* are the *means* that empower your spirit to meet these goals.

Are we still together? Have we clarified your understandings of The Essential Foundations? Do they make sense to you? Do you see how they satisfy *fundamental needs*?

Consider for a moment your position of leadership. Are you a parent? A business owner? A bus driver? A banker? Do you see how *FaithSkills* can help you to achieve your goals, regardless of your position? Have you already developed some of them? Would you like to strengthen others?

Remember – you're not expected to master all of the 13 *FaithSkills* at the same time, nor by any deadline. This process requires personal, positive change. These changes are the *doorways* or points of transition which lead to *permanent success*es. They may occur slowly at first, but will likely speed up as you become more accustomed to the patterns required for reaching your goals of permanent success.

Now, the bonus of developing a *FaithSkills* Personal Operating System is that you will develop *virtues*.

Had you ever considered that virtues are the result of an organized, ordered

Focus Box

My thoughts...

process of learning? It's a new perspective, isn't it? But that's what happens when you develop *FaithSkills*. You touch other people's spirits, and thus, their lives, for good.

Did you reflect upon the virtues of Discernment, Self-reliance and Patience that were mentioned in Chapters 4-7? Did you consider how they've influenced your life in the past when they've come through someone else's actions?

Can you see how developing these virtues could impact your life? Would they change the way you deal with people? Would other people change their attitudes towards you? Would they affect the decisions you make and the results you achieve?

As you've considered these new concepts and reflected upon them, you may have had moments when you felt guilt over past situations because you didn't do the now *evident* right thing.

Don't do that to yourself!

There's no room for guilt in a Sage's life – it's destructive. Remember that most of us try to do our best with the knowledge we have at the time. Now that you have different understandings, you may make different choices – that's growth. Don't dwell on the past. *Move forward*!

Take a good look at the chart on the following page. It summarizes the interrelationships amongst the needs, foundations, skills and virtues discussed in Chapters 4-7. Notice that we placed the first Foundation at the bottom so that all others build upon it.

The Success Building Process of Virtues

As you satisfy the Fundamental Need of:	Through the Essential Foundation(s) of:	By Exercising the FaithSkill(s) of:	You Build the Virtue of:
	Opposition	Fearlessness	PATIENCE
Harmony	Balance	Cooperation	
	Purpose	Devotion	SELF-RELIANCE
Knowledge	Order	Obedience	DISCERNMENT
Acceptance	Organization	Stewardship	

We hope we have given you an opportunity to assess your own progress to date. Understanding is a process. It requires putting knowledge into practice in order for it to be fully absorbed and adhered to.

Take your time in reviewing the material. Reflect on how it can improve your life. Consider how you will apply it to get the full impact of these pearls of success.

Now, let's move on to the next chapter. It's different and refreshing. It will likely give you much cause for reflection as it discusses the *Identifying* Foundations – those that explain who you really are.

Pro-Active Reflection

CHAPTER

9

Who Am I?

*T*he adrenaline was flowing. I couldn't believe my eyes. This was the most unbelievable circumstance of my career. I was in the coach section of a plane sitting beside William Andersen – an incredibly famous businessman with amazing leadership skills. He had huge assets – one of them was this airline!

Never in my wildest dreams did I ever think I would feast my eyes on my secret mentor, much less talk to him, yet, here I was. This would be the best five hours I'd ever spent on an airplane. My thoughts raced with a million questions I'd like to ask him.

I quickly stole another glance at him. Mr. Andersen was certainly not physically imposing in any way. He was only about 5' 8" tall – maybe 160 pounds: the exact opposite of what I'd pictured.

But it was his presence that intrigued me – it was amazing. I felt a warmth and calmness about him that had already put me totally at ease; I didn't feel the least bit intimidated by this important man.

Suddenly, he looked at me and smiled. I realized that I'd been staring at him for some time. I quickly turned my attention to my satchel and busied myself with finding my day timer notebook. For a time, my thoughts focused on my day's appointments and the details they entailed.

About half an hour later, I dared to steal another glance at Mr. Andersen. To my amazement, he was writing in what appeared to be a diary. Wait a minute. I was confused. Why would a multi-millionaire guru, a siren of wisdom like my secret mentor, a man's man as I pictured him to be – why would he be writing in a diary? I couldn't believe it. And another thing – if this guy actually owned the whole company, what the heck was he doing riding in the coach section?

I guess this guy isn't who I thought he was. What a let down. Oh, well, it had been a great rush while it lasted – kind of like the ones I got when I closed a deal or went over 3 miles on the treadmill – all temporary.

Time for a drink. The flight attendant suddenly arrived at our row. She leaned over to the look-alike and said, "Hope you enjoyed the takeoff, Mr. Andersen. Can I offer you a drink?"

"Thank you, Christine, I most certainly did. Please tell Captain Harris that I admire his expertise. I would love a club soda with a twist of lime. If you have a Clamato on the dolly, I'd appreciate a glass of that too, please."

"And what could I offer you, Miss?"

My mouth suddenly froze – I couldn't say a thing. My jaw must have dropped too, as I noticed the flight attendant staring at me. She nudged me and repeated, "Miss, can I get you something from the beverage tray?"

"Uh, yes, a diet coke, please." She could see that I was stunned. I tried to keep my composure but I couldn't – I was shocked.

What I'd felt. What my instinct had told me. My eyes were correct. This was THE MAN.

Without even realizing it, my aggressive nature kicked in and my tongue started wagging – I'd lost any potential for politeness.

"Mr. William Andersen, what are you doing riding coach when you own the whole company?" I slapped my hand over my mouth. My face was scarlet with embarrassment. How could I have been so rude? Before I could apologize, he turned to me and smiled.

"I do this all the time. It keeps me close to the pulse of the company. Thank you for asking. Evidently you know who I am. May I ask with whom I have the pleasure of sharing the next few hours?"

"Bobbie Seles, sir. I'm terribly sorry for my rudeness."

"Oh, no. I don't think that was rude at all. Actually, it was quite entertaining and refreshing to see such spontaneity. So what is it that takes you across the nation today, Bobbie?"

The conversation was friendly. I was amazed at how comfortable

I felt talking to him.

The drinks arrived. We ended our exchange and turned to our own rituals and preparations.

When I glanced over again, he was writing in the same book I'd noticed before. This time, I just had to ask.

"Mr. Andersen, I couldn't help but notice that you keep a diary. I don't mean to be nosy, but it seems like an odd thing for one of the world's most influential men to do. You know, it's just not what one would think you have time for."

"Well, that's very perceptive of you, Bobbie, and by the way call me Bill" he said as he put the diary aside. "It's actually a journal. I agree that it wouldn't be considered normal if you didn't think that knowing who you are was important to you."

"I beg your pardon?"

"You see, a wise old man once told me that you can't know where you are, if you don't know where you've been. That's why I've kept a journal for the last 12 or so years. It helps me to exercise the powerful skill of reflection."

Bill stared off into the open cabin. "It's fascinating to look at how you become who you are. After all, that's what this whole experience we call life is all about, isn't it? Figuring out who we are, or, is it who we can become?" he asked, with a gleam in his eye that told me he knew something I didn't.

My intuitions were telling me that I was about to learn a lot more than I anticipated, but it wasn't going to be what I expected. Here I was, prepared to drill this man about the secrets of business success, yet, we were talking about our identities.

I cautiously responded. "I guess so – we're all trying to become someone – especially someone like you, rich and famous and all. But how does a journal help you do that?"

"Well, when I write in my journal, I document what I've discovered about myself. I write about the new knowledge I've gained through my daily activities. When I reflect, I often go back and read my writings – I see how my spirit has discovered its intelligence – how I've evolved, if you will. I demonstrate who I am and what I've progressed to through my daily actions as a person. After all, what we are today is the sum of what our thoughts have created, don't you think?"

"Yes, I do believe that that is true. However, aren't we more than just our thoughts?"

Bill responded with a matter-of-fact statement, "Absolutely. We're spiritual beings having a physical experience." His eyes peered deeply into mine as he said this. He clearly wanted to know how his statement had affected me. I'm sure my eyes told him the whole story. It had impacted me alright – far more than anything I'd ever heard before.

I sat back in the comfortable seat and relaxed. I knew that I was in the presence of a wise man, a Sage. His humility was evident and certainly unexpected, yet very refreshing. I was going to be taught on a level I'd never experienced before and I was totally at ease with the prospect.

Bill continued, "People are so misled in this life. They have the attitude that success is all about toys, riches, and fame. But when all is said and done, and bugs are gnawing at our bodies 6 feet under, what good are they? All we can take with us is ….."

"Our thoughts, I guess," I blurted out, "and our spirits, if you believe in that stuff."

"Absolutely," said Bill. "You can rest assured that as surely as we have a mind, we also have a spirit. We're spiritual beings. It's the spirit that allows us to experience this life so fully. You see, with our minds, we discover the intelligence that's within us. With this awareness, we go through life. We have experiences, through our bodies, that help us define our spirits. We discover our true identities, and most importantly, what we can become."

This was deep, but it felt good to me. It was something I hadn't ever considered before. To be sure I'd understood, I repeated to Bill, in my own words, what I thought he'd said.

"If I understand you correctly, what you're telling me is that we discover our intelligences with our minds. Then the experiences we have through our bodies help us to understand more about our spirits."

"Correct."

"So, do we all have the same intelligence to discover?"

"Yes and no."

I was confused.

Bill paused for a moment, then said, "Let me explain it this way. What are thoughts? How do you think we form our thoughts, Bobbie? Where do they come from? If you weren't a being of intelligence, how could you have an idea without anyone else being involved in its creation or insertion into your mind? Yet, when you share the idea, it can be understood by others, without you having to fully explain it. They will be able to understand it on their own. Most human beings have this ability, so we share a *common intelligence* in this way."

"We also share a common mass of intelligence related to such things as living, eating and sleeping – the survival skills."

"But we have differences too – they're what make us so unique and interesting. Through experience, we discover our individual natures and what drives us in our learning methods, as well as our learning interests. Thus, your intelligence and mine become different."

"I never thought about it that way," exclaimed Bobbie. "Does that explain why you're so successful, while many others are not so blessed?"

"Very good question, Bobbie. It's exciting to see you thinking through these things. You're mining your intelligence, if you will. Now consider this thought. We existed as spirits before we came to this earth. In this form, we could proceed only to a certain point in our discovery process, and then we needed to come here to obtain physical bodies so that we could continue with the process."

"While here, we have experiences that teach us about ourselves. Some people discover things about themselves that they don't like, so they make changes that begin a life-long improvement process. Others simply accept what they discover; they are content to remain as they are."

"That is why we have such incredible variations of people in this wonderful world. That's what makes this experience we call life such an exciting one. Some of us choose to perfect solid fundamentals in this life, while others prefer to proceed without them."

"Thanks to the help of my sage mentor, I decided to try to perfect the fundamentals in my life. That's why I've been so blessed as you say. My disciplined obedience to the fundamentals has helped me to be permanently successful beyond my wildest dreams."

Jackpot! I thought to myself. There are secrets to success. I knew it. I just needed an icon like Bill to explain them to me. Success, here I come!

Bill continued, "Bobbie, we've talked a little about success, but what do you think it is?"

Wow! Was he reading my mind?

"I think it's moving to the top of your chosen field – making good money, winning awards – you know, that kind of stuff."

"A lot of people would agree with you, but ….."

"Well," interrupted Bobbie, "if what you've achieved isn't classified as success, then I really don't know what true success is."

"You're right Bobbie. You don't know."

I was taken aback by the forthrightness of his statement. "Are you saying you're not successful?"

"According to the world's standards, I am, but only if you speak of success as a destination, not a journey."

"Well, Mr. Andersen, I guess I can see what you're saying. So many successful people that I know seem to be unhappy with their lives. They get what they want and then choke on it for the rest of their lives. Obviously, they don't understand what you've said about success being a journey – more of a process, I guess. So why haven't you ended up miserable?" I asked Bill. "Looks to me like you've got the excitement level of a 6-year-old on Christmas morning."

"Thank you for the compliment, Bobbie. I truly do feel like life is a continual Christmas morning. I am constantly discovering who I am, but most importantly, who I can become."

"You see, I've become sage about success. I've understood that success is fulfillment – balanced fulfillment – exactly as my sage mentor taught me."

"When I am fulfilled, my spirit rejoices, regardless of the nature of the situation. It could involve closing the next deal, creating a new airline, or seeing the smile on my secretary's face when she opens her birthday present.

Some people would call these adrenaline rushes; I call them fulfillment."

"Whenever we experience those feelings, we are experiencing success. Growth isn't a destination – it's a process. As you said, Bobbie, that's also what success is – a process."

"So then it's safe to say," I stated, "that success isn't anything tangible, is it? Success is an emotion, an experience, an …"

"A spiritual experience," Bill interjected. "Success is something we feel beyond our physical being. True success in itself is an affirmation that we have a spirit. As a matter of fact, it's the #1 need of our spirit. Do you believe that, Bobbie?"

"What? That we have a spirit?"

"Yes."

"I believe that there is a spirit within us," I replied, "otherwise how could you explain what happens to us when we do things we can't explain physically? Like when we get moved by music – nothing like a great dance beat to move you to your feet.

"But what is a spirit? Is my spirit different than yours?"

"Absolutely," exclaimed Bill, "our spirits are as different and unique as we are in our physical realms. As a matter of fact, our bodies are mirrors of our spirits."

This information sounded strangely familiar. Yes, I already knew something about my spiritual side. Tragedies of the past had made me all too aware of the deep emotions we can feel through our spirits. Love, fear, marriage, divorce, promotions and firings were some of the many experiences that had witnessed to me that we're much more than animals trying to survive.

But what makes us so different? Why is it that dogs, cats and other animals seem to have it all organized? They're born, they survive, they reproduce, and they die. The circle seems to be clearly established for them, but not for us.

We seem to have a *will* that dictates our passage. What Bill was saying to me made sense. It felt comforting, but what was I feeling?

Bill was staring into my eyes, waiting for me to return to the conversation. He knew. He sensed that I wasn't quite there. He knew I was reflecting upon his words. I was validating them, but how?

As I refocused into his eyes, Bill smiled and asked, "Have you ever considered how you could be more than one person at the same time?"

"I beg your pardon – that's impossible!" I retorted.

"Really?" he asked, as he placed his chin in his hand. "Let me ask you this. Are you not a daughter, a friend, a colleague, a stranger, and possibly a sister, an aunt, a niece or a competitor to someone at this very moment?"

"Yes," I said slowly, "you're right. I'm all of those at one time, and possibly more."

"Exactly. Just as we can *play* many different roles at the same time, so can we be *composed*, if you will, of more than one part at the same time, namely, intelligences, spirits, and bodies. Our intelligences evolved and were then formed into spirits that are

118

presently in this world possessing these beautiful creations called bodies. We are then capable of discovering more about who we really are, as we mentioned before."

Bill could see that I was a bit puzzled. "Let me show you something," he said. "My sage mentor used this illustration to help me understand this incredible fundamental."

He sat up straight in his seat and extended his arm, pulling back his shirtsleeve.

"Think about it this way. Look at my hand. Imagine it to represent the spirit. Let's say it isn't visible to us, but it represents what the intelligence has progressed to. The body is like a glove that fits perfectly over the hand."

Bill pretended to place a glove over his hand. "Even though the gloved hand still looks much like the ungloved hand, it now has different features, just like the body. It provides benefits to us in this life. However, the most exciting part is that the body outwardly shows the characteristics of the unseen intelligence and spirit – much like the glove does the hand."

"Every experience here allows us to further discover who we are, and what we're made of. As we discover, we gain knowledge, which allows us to grow. As we grow, we change. As we change, we experience fulfillment, which in this life, we call success."

My mind was racing as I tried to absorb what Bill had shared. I was trying to listen to all of this with my *heart*. I felt that what he had told me was true. It made sense. It was an orderly, logical explanation for what I could not explain, yet something for which I had fervently searched. But it seemed too organized, too perfect.

My mind wanted to challenge what he was saying, but my heart felt warmth and comfort. I pondered for a long time. I wrestled with my ideas and feelings. I remembered the impression I had had several hours before – the one about how I was about to learn more than I'd bargained for. This was a full load, yet why did it feel so right?

Many past events in my life flashed through my mind. With this new perspective, I now understood why certain things had occurred and why I had reacted the way I had. I realized how I could have reacted differently and changed the results of those situations.

I felt like this was one of those moments we all have at one time or another – private, solemn moments of growth when deep learning occurs – life-changing moments. I'd been touched to the core, which I now knew was my spirit.

As I reflected on the past, I could clearly see that whenever my spirit had been *touched*, my life had changed. My spirit was indeed an intricate part of me.

My entire essence knew that what he had told me was true. "I understand what you've told me, Mr. Andersen, but it's an awful lot to consume at one sitting."

"Not if you're ready for it," explained Bill. "Although our minds are capable of absorbing a great deal of knowledge, our intelligences are infinite in range. Thus, it's our purpose to discover our potential and expand it. So if you're ready for what I've told you, and I believe you are, you'll be able to grasp all that I've shared with you."

"Thanks for the vote of confidence. To tell you the truth, I think I have absorbed what you've told me, but I also think that this is a never-ending process in itself."

"You're absolutely correct, Bobbie," mused Bill, "I continue to absorb it every day since my mentor shared it with me."

"You said earlier, Mr. Andersen, that this mentor shared fundamentals with you. Tell me, what are they?"

His next statement surprised me.

"Evidently you possess the most valuable asset we can all have, Bobbie – you possess desire: a strong desire, as a matter of fact. I sensed it as you first settled into your seat and began assessing me."

I smiled sheepishly – I'd hoped he hadn't noticed.

"Your every action portrays a person with purpose," continued

Bill. "You pay close attention. You're diligent. It pleases and honors me to fuel that desire by answering your question."

Bill then shared with me The Essential Foundations of a sage life. He told me that as I utilized these Essential Foundations to orchestrate my own personal discovery, that I would not only grow tremendously, but I would be able to create permanent success beyond my present dreams.

He further explained that implementing The Essential Foundations would lead to the development of *FaithSkills*, as well as associated virtues. I would then be able to live a sage life – one that exemplified True Leadership skills – the basis for achieving great successes.

As I reflected on this intriguing information, Bill opened his journal and took out a piece of paper. He handed it to me as the plane prepared to land. It summarized everything we'd been discussing. I was hesitant to accept it, but he insisted.

He smiled again and said to me, "It's been my honor to share my sage learning with you, Bobbie. You are a motivated learner. I have great confidence that you, too, will become sage, and go on to achieve success in all aspects of your life."

"That's what this paper is," said Bobbie. "I'd like to share it with you, my son."

William, her 16 year old son, came closer to the reading desk where I was sitting.

"This document has guided me through all of my life to date. That day on the plane, William Andersen, one of the humblest men I've ever met, gave me the greatest gift I could ever have wished for – knowledge. He taught me who I was, and most importantly, how to become all that I desired to become."

"So why didn't you become the president of your own multi-national conglomerate – the one you planned even before you met Mr. Andersen?" asked William.

"Part of being sage is discovering what really counts as fulfillment in life. You need to find out who you are before you can truly find permanent success. The multi-national wasn't for me. However, I did reach tremendous levels of achievement, wouldn't you say?"

Young William glanced at the wall full of awards and family portraits. "Absolutely, Mom. Besides, if you'd been the president of that company, you may not have had time to have me."

Bobbie laughed and gave him a hug. "You're a great kid, William! You're a motivated learner, just as I was that day. That's why I shared with you what Mr. Andersen taught me so long ago. I took advantage of the Teachable Moment, as he called it, to help you understand important fundamentals that can lead you to achieve success. Read this document often. Read it whenever you seek to know how to discover *who you are*.

We've attached a copy of what the Sage, William (Bill) Andersen, gave Bobbie that day on the plane.

The Governing Laws

Sages know that in order to understand what we can achieve, and thus, become masters of our own destinies, we must first discover and apply the governing laws that empower us to meet our goals. This knowledge and its diligent implementation will ultimately ensure permanent success that will survive through time and all eternity.

These Governing laws are known as The Essential Foundations. They are named such because permanent success cannot be achieved nor maintained without diligent adherence to them.

Sages will organize their lives in order with purpose. They will do so by fully respecting the need for opposition in order to achieve the necessary balance to exist in harmony with the elements of this life.

Sages know that they are spirits having a physical experience. As they reflect, they discover the intelligence they possess, and thus, begin to discover who they are. This mortal experience is one of discovery and also of preparation for the next step in our progression.

Sages know that they have agency to take action through the laws that maintain this existence we call life. All successes in this life are directly predicated upon disciplined obedience to laws. As we perfect our understanding of these laws with the Essential Foundations, we can become humble, and if we do, we will orchestrate a bountiful harvest for ourselves.

Our harvest whether tangible or intangible, will be directly proportionate to our degree of commitment to these Essential Foundations.

Practical Faith is the power that Sages use to exercise these fundamentals through their spirits and into their lives.

123

Pro-Active Reflection

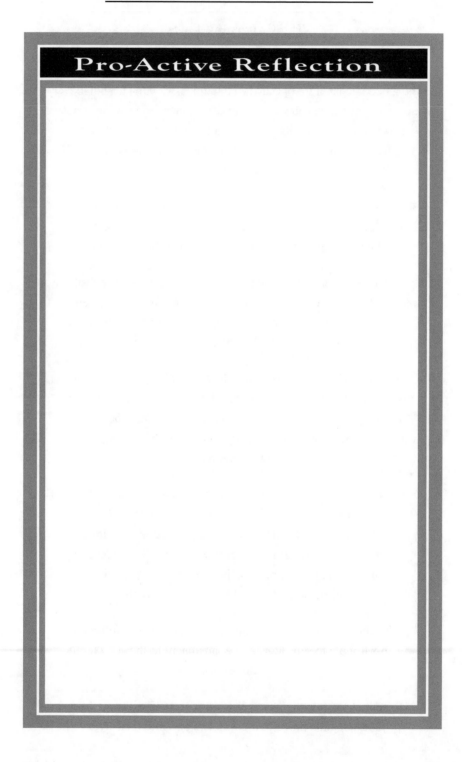

CHAPTER

10

Do You Recognize?

"Bobbie's Teachable Moment"

*I*n this wonderful story, we listened to a true Sage with an enormous understanding of who he really is. His mentor had helped him find solid answers to the question every one of us asks ourselves at some point in our lives – Who Am I?

These answers satisfy Our *fundamental need* for **identity**.

Interestingly, that wasn't the question for which Bobbie wanted an answer, or was it?

She wanted to know how she could attain the *"success"* that Bill possessed. At first, she perceived it as a tangible item – a possession to obtain – or a goal that had to be achieved. However, she quickly realized, and hopefully you did too, that Bill's greatest success was in knowing who he really was.

Once he discovered this deep *understanding*, he was able to further explore and develop skills that satisfied his fundamental needs. In the process, he became very influential.

As Bill taught Bobbie the skill of reflection, we too, could relate to the discoveries she was making about herself, as she looked proactively upon the actions of her past, and of course, the

Ponder This

Business Owners/ Operators:

Have you found yourself wondering if you'll ever achieve the level of satisfaction you thought you'd get from owning a business? You won't, if you're like Bobbie was before she met William. When you're on *the treadmill of successful*, in that you see success as an accumulation of objects, status or goals, you will never gain the fulfillment your spirit yearns for. Maybe it's time to stop and reflect in a way you couldn't without this new knowledge and ask yourself why did I go into business in the first place. Was

Continued next page...

> ### Ponder This
>
> it for the money, or for the freedom to exercise your agency? If it was both, which one dominates? They can't be of equal importance – *To thine own self be true.*
>
> If it's money, I can assure you that you'll never get enough. If it's freedom, or the empowerment that comes with exercising your agency, then look at your Personal Operating System to see if it's driven by money, and not your real desire – nothing like chasing your tail to get you confused. Stop and reflect from deep within yourself. Know your heart and you'll be amazed to see that the mind will always follow!
>
> Now This is Progress!

currents that drove them.

Bobbie sensed that what she was being told was true because it *resonated* a familiar tone within her. She was comforted with the pearls of wisdom that Bill was sharing because she allowed herself to use her entire being – her intelligence, spirit and body – to assess the validity of what she was being told. Isn't that the only way we can ever really *know* when something is true?

It touched Bobbie so deeply that she named her son after her mentor to sustain her fond memory of this Teachable Moment.

Now that Bill has shared these insights, you know how to verify that what you've read to date is correct.

Firstly, you must examine it in your mind to validate its intellectual merit.

Secondly, you must *reason* over it, or in other words, present the knowledge to your spirit.

Thirdly, you must filter it through your spirit.

If the information is true, or correct, you will have clear thoughts in your mind and warm feelings in your heart.

Try it. You'll know.

This process will indeed help you realize that you are a spiritual being having a physical experience.

Pro-Active Reflection

CHAPTER

11

The Day of Reckoning

*C*ranberries! Why did I ever get into this business? No money. Big mortgage. Huge bills. What's the point? It's one headache after another!

Robert sat down dejectedly on the tailgate of his pickup. What am I doing wrong? I've been at this business for 3 years and still haven't produced a crop that's up to industry standards. I was sure I'd be successful – after all, I spent two years at college studying about all of this – I even graduated with honors. I obviously know what to do, so what's the problem?

He wasn't looking forward to tomorrow when he had to submit the sum of his harvest to the juice plant. It'll only be another brutal day of reckoning, he thought.

The next morning, Robert met up with his crusty old neighbor, Cyrus, who also produced cranberries for the juice plant. He probably hasn't had much luck either, thought Robert. He doesn't even have the equipment I have, much less the training.

Robert hesitantly walked over to the clerk's office to submit his tally sheet for payout – he shuddered to think about it. As he waited, he couldn't help but eavesdrop on the conversation between Cyrus and the clerk.

"Gee, Cyrus, not quite as good as last year, but still the best yield per acre we've had this year. But that's not new for you, is it? You're always our top producer. We appreciate your loyal support of our plant, year after year. Thanks for another outstanding harvest."

Robert was shocked. He couldn't believe what he'd just heard. How could a crusty old man who just played at farming do better than someone who had the latest equipment and training? It didn't make sense. What does he know that I don't?

As Robert handed in his own tally sheet with its dismal numbers, he was totally embarrassed and frustrated. He debated about talking to Cyrus. Why should I have to? The guy isn't even in my league, he thought. He's old. He has no formal training. He probably wouldn't understand the methods I use. But, on the other hand, he's a lot better cranberry farmer than I am. I hate to have to admit that, but it's true. So, do I ignore him and continue on with my dismal results, or do I see if he'll share what he knows?

Robert slowly walked over to the clerk's office where Cyrus was standing. "Hey, Cyrus, my name is Robert Hancock. I'm the neighbor living just south of your property."

"I know," said Cyrus, as he peered up to Robert's 6 foot 4 inch height.

Robert felt about 5 feet tall at that moment. He debated about continuing the conversation, but reminded himself that he had nothing to lose.

"Cyrus, I couldn't help ……"

"I've met your son, Billy," interrupted Cyrus. "He's told me all about you and your family. Wonderful boy you have there. How old is he?"

"He's six," replied Robert. "You know, Cyrus, I couldn't help but overhear your conversation with the clerk when you handed in your tally sheet. It sounds like you're quite an accomplished producer for this plant."

"Well, that's what they tell me. I just do the best that Mother Nature lets me do and that seems to be the best they get."

"What do you mean?" responded Robert. "How does that happen when you don't even have the latest training or equipment?"

"All I know is that I know how to use the basics and that's all I've ever done. I simply obey the laws of Mother Nature."

This was not at all what Robert had expected to hear. Now what? Humility had never been one of his greatest attributes, but if he wanted to get himself out of this farming mess, he'd need to come up with some.

He followed Cyrus as he shuffled over to the clerk's office.

Robert cleared his throat and asked the question he'd been dreading, "Would you be willing to teach me what you do so I can reap the results you have?"

Cyrus smiled up at Robert. Actually, it was more of a smirk than a smile. He had wondered how long it would take for this conversation to happen.

"Sure," replied Cyrus. "But there are conditions. First, you have to humble yourself – I guess you've already started that part. Next, you can't criticize my techniques. I don't want to hear any high falutin' language from that College of yours."

Boy, I didn't realize I'd had that effect on old Cyrus, thought Robert. I've been quick to judge him – sounds like he knew that. But, my intuitions tell me that I can learn from this crusty old guy – probably more than I ever learned from college.

"Agreed," said Robert. "I'm the passenger – along for the ride. When can we start and how long will it take?"

"How about right now?" asked Cyrus, as he folded up his check and carefully placed it into his dusty old wallet. "If you buy me a coffee and a piece of pie over at the diner, I should be able to tell you all you need to know."

"Alright," said Robert in a playful tone, "let's head over there. Promise me you won't have seconds."

"I will if you don't listen carefully so that I don't have to," barked Cyrus.

Robert jumped into his new Ford pickup – a financed luxury – while Cyrus shuffled across the street to the diner where he'd parked his Mercedes. Cyrus always parked at the diner on cash-out week. He liked to celebrate his success by treating himself to a piece of Mollie's fresh cranberry pie with 2 heaping scoops of vanilla ice cream.

This year, it would taste better than ever – he didn't have to pay for it.

As Robert drove into the parking lot, he couldn't help but stare

> ## Ponder This
>
> Isn't it interesting how quick we tend to *judge a book by its cover* when we live by a physical or intellectual Personal Operating System? Just as was the case with Robert we usually end up quickly discovering that people are much more than what our physical or mental abilities are capable of discerning. That's why we should always reason with our hearts before we feel with our minds as we discover the people of our lives.

at Cyrus as he took off his dusty old jacket and threw it into the trunk of his Mercedes. He pulled out a quality leather coat and threw it over his shoulder as he entered the diner.

Robert was totally confused. This guy was a complete anomaly. He looks like a bump on a log, but wears an expensive coat and drives a new Mercedes – one that he owns outright. To top it all off, he's going to tell me how to increase the efficiency of my entire production cycle – over pie and coffee. What have I done to myself?

It quickly became evident that Cyrus was a regular at the diner; this cash-out week was no different than any other. Cyrus's order was repeated by both the waitress and the cook as if it was the request for the envelope for the Academy Awards.

Everyone, except Robert, knew that this was a momentous time. For the 13th year in a row, Cyrus had been the top producer – today was a time for celebration. They brought out the whole pie with a sparkler on it.

Cyrus giggled with the glee of an 8-year-old. Everyone in the diner was boasting about his accomplishment. Many came over to the table to shake his hand and kid him about maintaining his top status.

Robert was slowly realizing that his opinion of this old guy had been completely wrong. For the first time, he was seeing Cyrus in a totally new light. He was respected and appreciated. Besides that, he had knowledge that Robert desperately needed, whether Robert wanted to admit it or not. It was time to exercise due diligence and listen to every word of sage advice that Cyrus was about to deliver.

Robert waited for the fanfare to subside.

"It's the water," said Cyrus as he began to sip his coffee.

"I beg your pardon?" said Robert.

"It's the water – I understand it – when it has to be used, and what its purpose is in the process of growing cranberries. You see, I understand that water is a fundamental factor in Mother Nature's cycle of growth.

We, as farmers, try to accelerate her process, but we need to remember that we must duplicate her, not replace her."

Cyrus had Robert's complete attention.

"I realized many years ago that water is a fundamental element and the sooner I understood how to use it, the sooner I'd become a successful farmer."

Cyrus stared at Robert. "Have you ever had one of those moments when you know you've got to make a choice – you know, a crossroad – where you gotta make a decision?"

"Sure have."

"You see, for 48 years my father owned the property that I live on now. He never understood how perfect our land was for cranberries. He thought it was only swampland – lots of people did. Compared to your land, I'm 20 feet below what many consider the correct elevation in this area to successfully grow crops, but I didn't let that stop me. I wasn't prepared to accept the poverty of my father, so I got my nose into as many growers' publications as I could find. Do you know what I discovered?"

"No," said Robert.

"Cranberries." Cyrus emphasized his point by carefully placing a plump berry on his fork. "You see, I discovered that my location near the river wasn't a curse, but rather, a blessing, if I had the right crop. Cranberries need lots of water, so our conditions fit the bill perfectly."

"So you got into cranberries," confirmed Robert, "but that still doesn't tell me why you're a top producer."

"Correct! You're paying attention," teased Cyrus. "Cranberries have a short growth cycle but they can tolerate quite heavy moisture – that's why we flood the fields to harvest the crop. Of course, you know this because of those courses you took at that fancy college."

Robert grimaced. Did Cyrus have to remind him?

"But what you didn't learn at that college, is that being 20 feet below the local area allows me to flood my fields whenever I want to harvest the crop quickly and effectively."

Robert sensed that the secret was about to be delivered. He leaned forward in his seat so he wouldn't miss a word.

Cyrus continued. "Most people have to pump the water into the fields to harvest their crops, like you do.

That can take several days with so many farms out there needing water. For *educated* folks like you, with your huge field, you've claimed a week."

"It takes me three days," responded Robert quietly.

"Well, I use one of Mother Nature's assets – the river. My father thought it was a curse, but he didn't understand how to use it. I got permits and built dykes to control the natural flow so I could re-direct her forces to rapidly flood my fields. It took some aggressive action – I moved mountains of earth onto my property so that at harvest time, I could save a few days waiting for water."

"I don't get it," Robert blurted out. "You save time harvesting the berries, but how does that increase your yield?"

"Simple," quipped Cyrus. "That way I get a few more days of actual growing time so that Mother Nature can pack those little berries full of juice."

Wow! Thought Robert. Why didn't I talk to this guy sooner?

"And you know what? I've understood this advantage so well that during these last 10 years when folks like you started to come into the area to hyper-farm, I dug me a series of reservoirs so I could drain my little field quicker – that often gives me one extra crop in the year."

"No wonder you produce more per acre than any other grower."

"You see, it's the water – I understand when and how to use it."

"Plus," commented Robert, "you made lemonade out of the lemons by choosing the right crop for the property you were supposedly *cursed* with. Right, Cyrus?"

"Yup. It may seem simple – it is – but don't think for one moment it's easy. It takes a lot of hard work and preparation to take advantage of Mother Nature's gifts."

"That's for sure," said Robert. "I'm impressed, Cyrus. You have an amazing handle on the laws of Nature and how to take appropriate actions to get her to work for you."

"Well, thank you, Robert," said Cyrus as he slid the check over to him. "I learned very early in life that you only get ahead when you play by the rules. So, the sooner you decide to learn them, the sooner you'll master them."

"I guess that's the most important part of winning, right?" asked Robert.

"Absolutely not!" barked Cyrus with the gleam of a child in his eye. "You've got to want it. You've got to make a decision that you want to master the rules and then go for it. Ya gotta wanna!"

Robert was totally impressed with the enthusiasm of Cyrus's comments, but it was his humble closing comments that impacted Robert the most.

"You know, Robert, you've got to have respect for the laws that govern us and Nature. You also need to exercise your will with solid actions."

"But, the most important secret I can share with you today is this – you've gotta have faith in yourself.

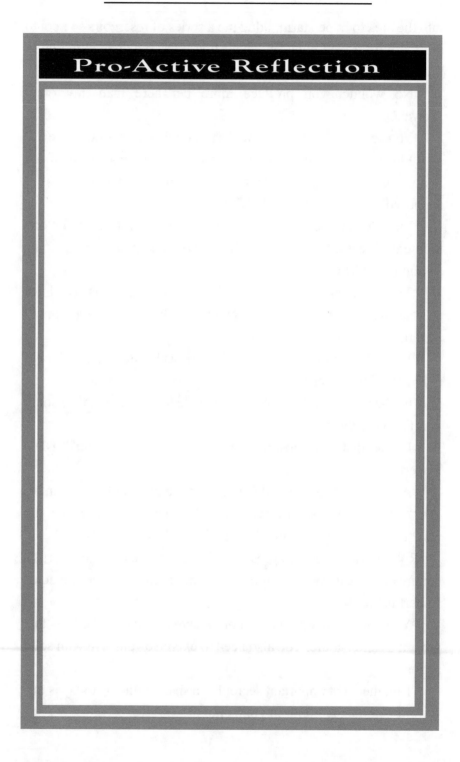

Pro-Active Reflection

CHAPTER

12

There's More To It Than You Think

"Robert's Teachable Moment"

*A*ll things in this world are organized into patterns. Laws provide the documentation or proof of this truth. Real laws, *governing laws*, are fundamental, unchangeable and self-fulfilling.

Laws are empowering – they are the instruments of success. The key to effective usage of them is to discover and understand the laws upon which your desired successes are predicated. Those who ignore this fact become victims of those very same laws.

We also need to exercise action in order to follow them. Laws are the patterns that allow us to apply our agency to the *fundamental* and *leveling foundations* you've already discovered.

When we act, laws become the justifiers and verifiers of our agency. If we don't act, we relinquish this agency and lose the empowerment that laws can provide to us – the laws then act upon us.

In our story of Robert and Cyrus, we see how laws, action and agency are interrelated and how one cannot function without the others.

Both men had their own understandings of these *empowering* foundations; each one used them in different ways to achieve the same goal of success.

Robert felt that his technical training and state-of-the-art equipment would give him an edge in the business of cranberry farming. Cyrus, on the other hand, used his own instincts and the natural resources available to him.

According to our knowledge of the backgrounds of these men, we might naturally expect that Robert would be the Sage, or the one with the most to offer about success in the cranberry growing business. However, we learn from this parable that being sage is not necessarily related to textbooks and schools, but rather to learning, understanding and applying certain fundamentals. Robert learned to acknowledge that Cyrus could offer more solid, practical advice related to these fundamentals than any College course he had taken, and he realized that possibly his own attitude towards his education blinded him from the practical understandings and skills it could provide him.

Let us consider Laws
the first of the empowering foundations.

Laws are essential to maintaining order. If we don't have them, or if we disregard them, or choose not to use them, we defeat our purposes and minimize our chances of reaching goals leading to success.

At the beginning of their conversation, Cyrus clearly explained to Robert his understanding of the fundamental nature of water and his conviction about imitating Nature's laws, not replacing them with his own. This understanding of laws fuelled his faith and reminded him that there are patterns to everything. He knew that his property could complete a pattern of some sort – he just needed to find out what it was.

Cyrus demonstrated his faith by researching his options to find a crop with growing requirements that matched the natural resources of his property. His understanding of the laws of water flow and their relationship to land elevation, together with his unquenchable desire to achieve success from a supposed curse, gave him a great advantage over surrounding cranberry farmers.

Reflect for a moment on your own respect for laws and we're not talking about the speed limit here. What part have they played in helping you achieve your current level of success? Do you recognize the patterns in those successes?

Sage entrepreneurs have learned from their own experiences, as well as those of others that disobedience stalls success. Thus, they search out and willingly obey the laws applicable to their particular circumstances. By their actions, they demonstrate the attitude that is built upon the foundation of law:

> "There's a Law Behind Every Success."

Think of a past experience where you or someone else wanted to achieve a particular goal but disregarded the *rules*, or *laws* related to it. What happened? How would the results, especially in the long-term, have changed if there had been an attitude of obedience?

How can obedience to laws empower you? What can you do to start making this happen so your rates of success increase? Jot down your thoughts in the box to the right.

This foundation satisfies another of our *fundamental needs* – the need for **direction**.

It is as necessary to our success as the other foundations that have preceded it. Every foundation is an integral part of the whole group – one building upon the other. If one is missing or incomplete, the strength of the whole is threatened.

Focus Box

My thoughts...

Let us now consider **Agency**
the second of the *empowering foundations*.

Agency is commonly thought of as the right to choose, however, it is more than that.

This process of choosing, or reasoning, can involve the intelligence and the body, but when it also involves the spirit, the entire being influences the choices. When we use our agency, we are consciously exercising our spirit's will to choose, which helps to satisfy our *fundamental need* for **empowerment**.

Choices can lead to positive or negative results. In our parable, we see examples of both.

Cyrus had learned years earlier that he could either choose to accept his father's attitude towards the land, or, he could exercise faith in himself and determine what actions he could take to make the laws of nature work for him, not against him. His research yielded practical information that guided him to choose a crop he hadn't previously considered – one that would help him be successful and avoid the poverty his father had known.

Robert, on the other hand, chose to go to college to learn about equipment and techniques that would make his farming efforts successful. His choice was logical and would seemingly help him achieve his goals.

Even though both Robert and Cyrus chose to obey laws, as they understood them, Cyrus's understandings developed intuitions that led him to stick to the basics of nature, rather than rely on *more advanced* methods.

The problem with Robert was that his understanding of the foundation of laws was incomplete. He understood the newest laws of technology, training and methods, yet missed an absolutely basic fundamental that successful farmers must understand – how to effectively correlate water usage with the layout of the land.

Without all of the necessary information, he couldn't effectively use his agency to achieve the successes he desired.

As a developing Sage, you are learning that life is about choices – whether simple or complex, they need to be made.

Sages live by the attitude that:

"Choose or Don't Choose – Either Way, You Choose."

Wise individuals recognize that inaction is, in itself, the exercise of will.

By learning to apply this foundation of agency, you will be able to make educated, informed choices that represent your will – you will also be able to discern when these are required.

Sage individuals understand the principle of agency and valiantly exercise it in their varied leadership roles.

They boldly proclaim their intentions and act upon them because they have deep spiritual confidence – faith – in themselves. Their team members recognize these qualities and rely on Sages to lead them to success.

Why is the ability to choose so important to your success? How can

Focus Box

My thoughts...

147

Focus Box

My thoughts...

you use your knowledge of the Essential Foundations to improve your ability to make choices?

Let us now consider **Action** the third of the *empowering foundations*.

If you don't take action in this life, life will act upon you. Cyrus understood this truism. He had seen what his father's lack of action had done to him, and he did not want to repeat it. Once he made the choice to grow cranberries, he took the actions necessary to make it a successful venture. He moved mountains of earth to build dykes to redirect the flow of water to serve his purposes. He also built reservoirs.

Sages, like Cyrus, recognize the importance of taking actions that will fulfill their purposes. They understand the attitude that is built on this foundation:

"Push or be pushed."

How do you feel when you're pushed into something rather than making a choice for yourself? Do you now understand how and why this can happen? Do you see how using the foundations of agency and action together can empower you to avoid being *pushed*? Write down your ideas in the box to the left.

People of action are not victims. They don't sit back and wait for things to happen – they actively intervene in their own lives. They exhibit high levels of energy. They're encouraged that their efforts will lead them to success because they're built on the Essential Foundations.

The foundations of agency and action satisfy our innate *fundamental need* for empowerment – the opportunity for the spirit to exercise its will upon its environment.

As you already know, there are *FaithSkills* and *virtues* associated with each foundation. Thus far, we have introduced you to eight of the thirteen *FaithSkills*. These are Stewardship, Obedience, Devotion, Cooperation, Fearlessness, Reflection, Humility and Discipline.

The ninth *FaithSkill* of **Honesty** is related to the foundation of laws.

In our parable, Robert dreaded the thought of having to ask Cyrus his secrets, but he knew that he needed to understand what they were. Unless he honestly communicated that need and desire, his dismal results would continue.

Cyrus was most willing to tell Robert. He held nothing back, but told him precisely what he did to bring about success. His communication was honest, clear and complete. It was so honest that it sometimes cut deep to Robert's thoughts and heart.

Consider for a moment what would have happened if Cyrus had been dishonest. Some of us were probably thinking that he should have been, considering Robert's past attitude of pride and arrogance. At the very least, Cyrus should have withheld a portion of his knowledge, knowing that Robert might now have an advantage over

Ponder This

Parents –
allowing children
to exercise their
agency, within the
parameters you set,
helps in 2 ways:
1. they learn to
exercise faith in
their abilities by
using them to make
decisions, and
2. it improves their
self-esteem because
they discover that
they are capable of
making decisions,
good or bad, given
the opportunity to
prove it.

him. But he didn't.

As a Sage, Cyrus knew that the use of *FaithSkills* orchestrates a win-win situation for all concerned. He recognized that by sharing his knowledge honestly, he and Robert could have a mutually beneficial relationship instead of a negative, competitive one. Cyrus also understood another sage truism – you can't expect honesty if you don't give it.

Have you found yourself in circumstances that demanded honesty? Did your actions help or hinder the situation? How did you feel about yourself? Can you now more deeply appreciate how using this skill can provide long-term benefits in your life?

Isn't it interesting how observing the success patterns that someone else uses in their life can influence you to want the same in yours? Why? Because your spirit recognizes the positive results they generate.

Valiance is the *FaithSkill* associated with the foundation of agency.

At this stage of one's progress in developing his or her own *FaithSkills,* one appreciates the worth of the foundations and their associated *FaithSkills*, and thus becomes not only passionate about them, but also valiant in their implementation.

Sages are also valiant in defending agency and the empowerment it gives to others. They strive to avoid imposing their wills on others, but rather will coach others to appropriately exercise

...en helps a Sage to achieve success ...rs with their hearts, while managing ...s. This understanding is the very essence of *stewarding*. Sages know that others must be empowered to exercise their own agency.

Cyrus understood this. He wanted to help Robert understand that there were laws involved in growing cranberries and that he had to obey them if he wanted to be successful, but he never told Robert how to implement them – that was his choice.

You will remember that *stewarding* also fosters a *we* approach for the common good. Cyrus was willing to share his knowledge to help Robert, even though it might have affected his standing as the top grower. As a result, Robert felt a loyalty to Cyrus that would benefit both of them.

When you respect the agency of your team members, as well as your own, you build trust and loyalty that bonds. The kind that makes people want to contribute a better effort towards the success of all concerned. You, and everyone involved, know that you can depend on each other to make sacrifices, if necessary, to make this happen. It's possible and satisfying to experience!

The *FaithSkill* related to the foundation of action is **Authenticity.**

Cyrus didn't put on airs or try to be something he wasn't. He was an ordinary cranberry farmer who knew what he had to do to be successful and did it. He knew he was the top grower but never flaunted his success. Everyone liked him for who he was – plain, old Cyrus – nothing more, nothing less.

Sages appreciate people who are authentic. They then know what to expect from those around them.

Are you an authentic person? Have you ever previously considered how this skill could influence your life as a parent, teacher, employer or working professional?

Rene Says

Live a Genuine Life. Now that you know that you're a three-dimensional being and can develop physical, intellectual, or spiritual operating systems, it's easy to see that when you're intellectually based, you can justify being a different person depending on the circumstances in which you find yourself. You know, "I would never show that kind of behavior at home" or "I would never do that around so and so"? If another person, or the environment in which you find yourself can dictate the person that people see, who are you? Since we build our self-identities from the reflections we get from other people, how can you really know who you are when you give different impressions?
Continued next page...

Actions are often the result of what the heart believes and what the mind thinks. They speak a thousand words. Be authentic in all you do and people will be moved by your very presence.

Thus far, we've discussed eleven of the thirteen *FaithSkills*. We realize that it may be difficult for you to remember them all, so here's a quick review:

- Stewardship
- Obedience
- Devotion
- Cooperation
- Fearlessness
- Reflection
- Humility
- Discipline
- Honesty
- Valiance
- Authenticity

Don't worry, we'll provide you with lots of charts of all 13 later in the book.

Please remember that you are not expected to master them all at once! It's an on-going, life-long process. Life's many experiences will help you assimilate and refine them, one step at a time.

As I am sure you remember, *virtues* are also developed through the effective and Integrity.

The fifth *virtue* is **Honor**. It is related to laws.

Just as Cyrus understood that he had to obey the laws of nature to have success in his business, so you, as a developing sage entrepreneur, understand that you need to honor and obey the laws inherent in your endeavors if you are to achieve success. You can't *get around them* in any way if you are to reach your desired goals.

It is this disciplined obedience to what you know must happen that forms integrity, and in turn, Honor. People will perceive you as honorable and trust what you say and do.

Influence is the sixth *virtue*. It is associated with the foundations of agency and action.

Once Cyrus made his decision regarding which crop to grow, he obtained the necessary permits and disciplined himself to dig the dykes and reservoirs needed so the crop would succeed. He didn't wait for Nature, or someone else, to do it for him.

The results were incredible; they

It's duplicitous and confusing for you and for those who surround you. If you expect people to be genuine with you, be an example of the genuine person you seek to meet. Our spirits yearn for authenticity; they immediately recognize it when they witness it. No other style of living will more positively cultivate respect for you than that of genuine authentic actions and words. Trying to be what you think others want you to be, will never allow you to be who you really are. You should use the image reflected from others to guide, not dictate, your efforts to become what your heart strives for you to become – a genuine and *permanent success*.

influenced the entire farming community, especially Robert. When he saw what Cyrus had accomplished, he knew that this *"crusty old farmer"* had the answers he needed.

Think of someone who has had a profound influence on you. Does he or she exhibit the qualities we've discussed in this chapter? Would you like to have the same influence on others? Of course!

So why not start the process now. Take a moment to list some of the areas in your life that are in need of your improved *FaithSkill* of Obedience. There's nothing like the power of now!

CHAPTER

13

Sage Reflections

four chapters is new to many of you and for some may seem overwhelming! So, before we proceed any further, we want to reassure you that you are not alone in these feelings. This may be the first time that many of you have been exposed to such different perspectives. You will need time to digest them and determine how they can fit into your *auto pilot* behavior.

The chapter on the *Identifying* Foundations of intelligence, body and spirit may be the most unusual and perhaps the most difficult to absorb because it discusses ideas that are not concrete – you can't see, or touch, or taste, or smell the *intelligence* or the *spirit*. You can, however, feel their influences.

Could you identify with Bobbie's awakening experience as she talked with Bill? He opened her understanding to things that had always operated in her life, but she hadn't recognized them, or, if she did, she didn't know what they were.

Can you recall a life-changing experience – one where you felt that you would never be the same again? Why did you feel that way? What distinguished that experience from others you'd had? Would you say you were different because of something that happened deep within you – because your *spirit* was touched? Has this *changed feeling* remained with you? If so, it's because your spirit was involved.

As Bill explained to Bobbie, it is only through the physical body that the spirit can truly manifest itself.

Understanding the interrelationship among the spirit, body and intelligence satisfies our need to know who we truly are – it helps us to establish our unique identities.

However, if we hope to adequately meet this need for identity, we must have satisfied the 3 *fundamental needs* that precede this one, namely, Acceptance, Knowledge and Harmony; they build upon each other.

We've mentioned this point often – that the needs build upon one another, as do the foundations, skills and virtues. Is it becoming clearer to you why we say that? Think of a ladder. In order to use one effectively, you need to climb one rung at a time in consecutive order. The needs and foundations build upon one another in a similar fashion. The concepts and principles acquired at one level are necessary in order to have success at the next.

Think about it. Without an appreciation for acceptance, knowledge and harmony, you would have trouble comprehending or even considering the value of knowing the three dimensions of your being and the relationship they have with one another. Why? Because you first need to feel comfortable within yourself – in other words, satisfy your *inward* needs for acceptance, knowledge and harmony. Consider this situation. If, for instance, you struggle with feeling accepted at work, home, at the gym, or any other place, and most of your energies are consumed with meeting that need and thus accepting yourself, how can you focus on finding out who you really are, when you're not even comfortable with who you presently perceive that you are? An interesting thought, isn't it? Why not acknowledge your own deep need for acceptance first. Satisfy it by consciously starting the process, and then enhance the process by reading your reflection off of other people from the actions you have with them. Use your *spiritual glasses* to read those reflections and you'll be amazed to discover how invigorating this process of *self-esteeming* is.

You also discovered three new *FaithSkills* associated with the *Identifying* Foundations. They are reflection, humility and discipline.

You've probably realized by now that we've frequently encouraged you to use the skill of reflection. We hope that you're gradually feeling more comfortable with your ability to exercise it. It is more than just thinking; it involves putting yourself into a given this in Bobbie's story, you could follow her through her thought processes and get answers to questions that you may not have thought of yourself. Learning can happen by utilizing your own experiences or those of others. Reflection is an interesting method of self-examination, isn't it?

Do you now recognize what those *forces* are that act upon you and where they come from? It's amazing isn't it, how your *fundamental needs* act like currents on your daily actions. Imagine what you could do if you harnessed them through conscious application of these new understandings?

Humility is another *FaithSkill* that helps one to look inward. It may be defined as *teachability*, or a willingness to learn. Sometimes, we humble ourselves because we recognize the need. Other times, circumstances humble us – we may have little choice in the matter.

It takes humility to consider the perspectives we've presented, especially if they don't fit into what you already know and understand. You may be venturing out of your comfort zone by even considering these concepts and their application in your life. You're not alone. Many people are just beginning to discover that they too have a spirit that drives them. We applaud you for having enough faith in yourself to exercise the courage needed to explore these new frontiers. Your spirit won't regret it.

Discipline is the third *FaithSkill* that is developed through the *Identifying* Foundations.

What comes to mind when you hear the word discipline? A new diet that you're trying hard to follow?

A New Year's resolution that you've managed to keep? Keeping quiet when you really want to say something unkind? Going to work every day whether you feel like it or not?

Sages explain this word as follows: matching your physical

Rene Says

Discouraged? Have you ever wondered why it is so easy to get discouraged? I have. Remember that this world is not our natural state of existence. As spiritual beings having a physical experience, we're growing at a rapid pace. We want to learn about our identities and enormous capacities. Yes, it may seem simple but that doesn't make it easy; that's why we can get so easily discouraged, especially if we forget that we chose this path. It's natural for us to enjoy those moments of relaxation that allow us to shed the burden of the physical vessel we occupy in order to regain a sense of our natural state. Sadly, for many it is the desire for those

Continued next page...

desires with your spirit's needs, then channeling them in such a sustained way that, despite distractions, you can accomplish your goals. Does it sound easy? It's not!

Disciplining ourselves is probably one of the most difficult things we need to do while we're here. Everyone has areas to work on, but we use our agency to choose whether or not we will. Others can try to discipline us, but the most effective kind comes from within – only you can really discipline yourself – only I can truly discipline myself.

Reflect for a moment on these questions. Have you exercised self-discipline in the past? What circumstances determined the area in which you would focus? How did you begin the process? Did you always maintain your *self-control*? If not, how did you regain your determination to get back *on track*? It didn't happen overnight did it?

If you've had difficulty with developing this skill – we all have at one time or another – could it be that you confused your spirit's needs with your physical wants? Or, worse yet, did you allow your intelligence to justify your physical wants regardless of what your spirit said? No wonder discipline is hard to maintain.

162

following this step-by-step process that begins with satisfying the *fundamental need* for acceptance, and then building upon that success, need by need.

This book is presenting to you the fundamentals necessary for building that enduring, permanent success process.

However, you are the one that must absorb them. You are the one that must implement them if these successes are to occur.

The process is simple, but not easy. It's never-ending and ever-changing because circumstance, people, and needs are always changing. So don't be too hard on yourself at first, don't get discouraged with your efforts: patience will win this battle!

I can't emphasize this enough.

Now, you will recall that each category of Essential Foundations has its associated *virtue* or *virtues*. In the case of the *Identifying* Foundations, the virtue is integrity.

Do you value people with integrity? Is it because you know you can trust them? Can you rely on them to do what they say they're going to do? Will they defend their values despite outside pressures?

Are you a person of integrity? When

moments of comfort that allows them to blindly respond to the powerful allure of alcohol and drugs. You see, when under the influence of these awful vices, we deaden our physical bodies and gain a false sense of our natural state, or spiritual beings. Because many have forgotten their purpose, or are uncomfortable with the degree of difficulty that life's challenges have presented, they choose the path of denial and float through life unconsciously. Now that's discouraging. So, pick up your socks and take another step. It's a journey we're on and I've yet to see a trip without a valley or two. Remember – the greatest growth occurs in the valleys, not on the mountains tops.

163

thinking of you, could your family members and friends answer *yes* to the previous questions? If not, why not?

Perhaps there are weak rungs in your ladder of success. Maybe you need to work on being more obedient. Maybe you're not very good at achieving harmony in your life. Or, maybe you lack discernment or patience. All of us struggle with some or all of these things, in greater or lesser degrees. Often, it depends on the day and how things have unfolded. We can't *perfect* the virtues, but we can improve our knowledge and personal application of them.

Precisely.

That's what you're doing as you read about the *Empowering* Foundations of laws, agency and action and their associated *FaithSkills* and virtues. You're improving. New laws satisfy our *fundamental need* for direction – knowing how we're going to achieve our goals, while agency and action meet our need for empowerment, or the right to exercise our wills upon our environment.

Many people feel that laws exist to be broken and the trick to understanding laws is not getting caught. They also feel that if they can't see a justifiable reason for the law, they're excused from obeying it.

But, the fact is that there are laws, both written and unwritten, that govern literally everything in this life; the sooner we realize the rewards of obeying the laws that govern the successes we desire, the sooner we'll succeed – permanently.

What is your attitude to laws in general? Did you ever consider that there are laws that govern the successes you desired? Do you think now's the time to reveal and understand those governing factors? Consider the effect this could have on your level of achievement.

Honesty is the ninth *FaithSkill*; it is associated with the foundation of laws. By developing the previous *FaithSkills*, you have prepared yourself for this new one. Does this mean that you have perfected all previous skills?

No. It only means that you are increasing your capacity to discover, to learn, and to adapt this new *FaithSkill*. Remember – it's a process, much like climbing stairs.

> **Think about it**
>
> Parents, Business owners, mechanics, teachers – anyone in positions of leadership – you all need to have faith in yourself if you want to succeed. Otherwise, the spirits of those you lead have difficulties understanding you.

Reflect for a moment on the part that honesty has played in your life. How has it influenced the results of your life's experiences? If some were less than satisfactory, what needed to change to bring about more desirable results? It's pretty important isn't it?

The *FaithSkill* of honesty leads naturally into the *virtue* of honor.

Think of some people whom you would identify as honorable. How did they get that way? What characteristics do they portray? Are they also discerning, self-reliant people? Are they patient? Do they have integrity? Wouldn't it be interesting to know if they had also developed the skills we have discussed thus far? Likely so, in one degree or another.

This brings us to the sixth *fundamental need* – empowerment – being able to freely exercise our wills upon our environments. In order to do this, we need to have an understanding of the foundations of agency and action.

Agency gives us opportunity to make choices for ourselves. If you've ever had this privilege removed, even for a short time, you know the feelings of entrapment it generates. We're here to learn how to make choices and be responsible for the consequences of those choices. Remember that even if you think you haven't made a choice, you really have – you've chosen not to choose.

Does that sound like an oxymoron? It does, doesn't it? But it's true. Think about it. Agency is in constant motion – exercise it, or it

> **Remember This**
>
> The main function of the Essential Foundations and *FaithSkills* is to provide a doorway for satisfying our *fundamental needs*.

will be exercised on you. Use its power or lose its power. The way to effectively do this is through Valiance and Authenticity, the *FaithSkills* associated with the foundations of agency and action.

The Sages of the world are valiant in defending their causes. They have done their homework in terms of the previous needs and the foundations that relate to them, so they know what has to be achieved and how to go about it. They can stand firmly, because they know what they're doing.

At this point, we hope that your intelligence, spirit and body are in harmony as you develop your success building system. We also hope that your confidence level, or degree of faith in yourself, has been greatly enhanced.

Sage individuals have gone through this same learning and developing process that you are now undergoing. They understand that it is ongoing –improvement occurs one step at a time.

They also realize the great benefits of continually developing themselves. Many are recognized as great leaders that others are willing to follow. They are authentic – there is nothing *"plastic"* or *"put on."* They can be trusted and relied upon. Such traits instill confidence in team members and encourage them to rally around the leader. Sages like these are empowered with the virtue of influence. It is easy to see why.

Would you like to be seen as such a leader? Have you worked with someone who is? What would you have to do to become one? With *FaithSkills*, it's very *doable*!

Think of those who have had a great positive influence in your life. Do the characteristics listed above describe these people? Has their influence on you given you opportunity to influence others? In turn, have those people influenced others? It's a never-ending cycle, isn't it? Just like a rock that is thrown across a pond makes ripples for great distances, so the influence of others stretches far beyond immediate view.

Take a look at the chart below. It will summarize the information that we've presented thus far. We hope you are gradually feeling more comfortable with these new concepts and how they contribute to the successful development of your own *FaithSkills* Personal Operating System.

The Success Building Process of Virtues

As you satisfy the Fundamental Need of:	Through the Essential Foundation(s) of:	By Exercising the FaithSkill(s) of:	You Build the Virtue of:
		Authenticity	HONOR
	Action	Valiance	
Empowerment	Agency	Honesty	INFLUENCE
	Laws	Discipline	
Direction	Body	Humility	INTEGRITY
	Spirit	Reflection	
Identity	Intelligence	Fearlessness	PATIENCE
	Opposition	Cooperation	
Harmony	Balance	Devotion	SELF-RELIANCE
	Purpose	Obedience	DISCERNMENT
Knowledge	Order	Stewardship	
Acceptance	Organization		

The next two chapters will discuss the Essential Foundations that meet our *fundamental need* for fulfillment – namely, the harvest and commitment.

Pro-Active Reflection

CHAPTER

14

We Reap What We Sow

*G*arry tightened his tie and grabbed his suit jacket from the back of the swivel chair in front of his desk. He glanced at the clock. 1p.m. Friday afternoon office activities were proceeding as usual, but Garry was oblivious to them. His mind was obsessed with thoughts of his most important company assignment to date.

As he grabbed his car keys off his desk and headed for the door, his mind focused on the details – he'd lost count of how many times he'd thought about them. Flight out tonight. Meet with engineers tomorrow and Sunday to collect and test final data. Back Sunday night. Wrap up report. Presentation on Monday morning at 11.

He grinned as he thought about the ingenious experiment he'd devised to test the hypothesis. They said it couldn't be done, but he was about to supply data that would prove them wrong. If the board accepts this – no, wait a minute – *when* the board accepts this on Monday – I'll be set.

He was home before he knew it. As he opened the front door, his wife, Susan, glanced up. He sure looks happy, she thought. I wonder what's up.

Garry dropped his briefcase and spun her around in a tight hug.

"What's with you, Garry? You look like you just won a million dollars!" said Susan.

"Well, you never know – you never know," said Garry with a sly grin.

"C'mon, tell me!" begged Susan.

"As a matter of fact, I want to talk to you and the kids," said Garry. I have something to share. Brandon, Sarah," called Garry. "Could you please come into the family room? I'd like to tell you something."

Twelve-year-old Brandon and fourteen-year-old Sarah sauntered into the room.

"Hi, Dad," said Sarah. "What's up?"

"Well, guys," said Garry slowly. "You know that I've been out of town a lot this past few months, and even when I'm not, I've worked a lot of late nights."

"That's for sure," exclaimed Brandon. "It seems like we hardly ever see you. I feel like I don't have a Dad!"

"I know, son," said Garry. "But I've been working on a very important project that will help our family a lot. When the Board accepts my proposals on Monday morning, that means I'll be home a lot more. It will also mean that we'll have money to do some of those things we've talked about."

"But, Garry," said Susan. "How can you be so sure the board will accept them?"

"Well, because this time, I've prepared a lot better. I studied and learned about the important laws needed for the experiments. Then, I organized them in a way that the lab people would know how to work with them in the right order to achieve my purpose."

"What did you mean, Dad, when you said *this time*?" asked Sarah.

"I just meant that I had a good opportunity about four years ago, but, at that time, I didn't know much about the sage laws for success, so I blew it."

"Sage laws?" asked Brandon. "What are those?"

"They're fundamentals, or basic laws, that people need to obey if they're going to achieve success in any part of their lives – this includes school, work, and family life."

"How did you learn about them, Dad?" asked Sarah.

"Well," interjected Susan, "Dad was feeling really upset with himself when the other opportunity didn't work out, and he didn't know quite what to do. But he had a very good friend who understood the situation."

"That's right," said Garry. "He helped me to see that the failure I'd experienced wasn't the end of the world – even though at the time I thought it was. He said that this was called opposition, and that it was a necessary part of learning and growing. Everybody has to face it in one way or another."

"Kind of like when I want to watch my favorite TV show and Sarah wants to watch something different, so we argue about it?" queried Brandon.

"Yes," said Garry. "And what do you do to solve the problem?"

"We agree to take turns," said Sarah. "One night, he watches his show, and the next night, I watch mine. That works pretty good."

"So then you've brought balance back into the situation," explained Garry. "That's what my friend helped me to learn. Even though I'd *fumbled the ball*, so to speak, I needed to get back in the game. That's when I started looking for another project. My friend had coached me so well in cultivating the sage laws, that when I learned about this project, I knew that I could apply them and be successful. The first thing to do was thoroughly prepare. Then I could organize things in order to achieve my purposes, just like I told you a few minutes ago."

"Once you knew this stuff, Dad, was it easier to make the project work?" asked Sarah.

"Well, it was easier in one way because I knew exactly what fundamentals I had to obey, but that didn't mean that opposition left me alone. There were lots of problems at times: things like experiments that didn't work because somebody didn't follow directions, incomplete reports because the secretary was off sick for two weeks and the information wasn't passed on to her, the lab was without power for three days so experiments couldn't be done and we got behind schedule. There were many more issues, but thanks to my sage friend, I could think them through and get the experiments done, the reports fixed and generally work with my team of people to get things back into balance. I learned to trust my feelings the way I used to. For the most part, things worked out very well. Sure helped to build up my self-confidence!"

"So how will all of this help our family?" asked Susan.

The kids nodded. They had been wondering the same thing.

"That's the best part, guys," said Garry excitedly. "I've obeyed the sage laws. I've made good choices. I have great confidence that because of these things, the board will accept my findings. That means that I won't have to travel. I'll get to work normal hours and be home with all of you so we can do neat things together – we'll even have the money to do them."

The whooping and cheering from his family confirmed to Garry that the past months of sacrifice had been worth it.

He explained that he needed to make one more trip to finalize his preparations, but it would be the last one.

"Awesome! We're with you, Dad!" yelled Sarah.

"Good luck, Dad – we can hardly wait for you to get back!" shouted Brandon.

The smile on Susan's face was huge – this was going to be a good year!

Garry checked his watch. Almost time to leave for the airport, he thought.

He left his excited family and started towards the den to collect the maps he'd need to take with him.

Suddenly, he stopped abruptly, his smile frozen on his face. Oh, no! What have I done? The three pages of data from the first part of the experiment – they're still in the computer! Where am I going to get 2 hours between now and Monday to analyze them? Maybe I could leave them out? No way – they have to be there or the rest of the report doesn't make sense. How could I have been so stupid? I...

Hold it, Garry. This is not four years ago. You're a sage now, he reminded himself. Sages don't *lose it* at critical times. Calm down and think.

Maybe I could.....hey, wait a minute. Joan. Why didn't I think about her before? I've been so preoccupied with this project that I'm not even thinking straight. Teamwork – that's what this is all about! How could I have overlooked such a basic sage attitude? Joan is a critical part of the team, and I haven't even included her. But, time is of the essence. Is it too much to expect?

Garry reached for the phone.

"Hello. Joan? It's Garry. I have a huge favor to ask. I...."

Sunday night – already. It's done, thought Garry as he dropped his exhausted body into a seat by the window. It's been a long two days, but I've got everything. I can't wait to see the looks on the faces of those skeptics in the boardroom – they're going to be impressed.

Monday morning was rainy and cold as Garry left early for the office. No matter, he thought. Today is my day; I'm going to enjoy it.

As he walked into the office, his mind suddenly flashed back to four years ago. Instantly, his palms were sweaty – his stomach churned. What if Joan hadn't finished the analysis? What if....?

Joan's voice broke into his thoughts. "Here's the report, Garry! Time was tight, but I finished it early this morning before coming to work. I couldn't let you down!"

Garry wanted to hug her, sweaty palms and all. Faithful, dependable, committed Joan.

"What would I do without you, Joan? You're a lifesaver! When this whole thing is over, there's a bonus coming your way!"

"Awesome! Just don't forget to keep me on your team!"

"Absolutely! I couldn't do it without you!" exclaimed Garry.

For a moment, he thought about the sincere efforts he'd made to cultivate a solid working relationship with Joan. It had paid off in spades. They shared a mutual trust and respect that he'd rarely enjoyed in any previous work projects. The sage lessons of the past were paying huge dividends – far more than he could ever have imagined.

Garry smiled to himself as he thought about his sage mentor – I think he'd be proud of me!

Eleven o'clock soon arrived. Garry disappeared into the boardroom.

Several hours later, he emerged, carrying a pile of papers. The grin on his face said it all.

"They accepted it!" he yelled to Joan. "They bought the whole thing – every convincing, persuasive detail – they liked it all!"

"Of course they did, Garry! Why wouldn't they? You followed through on all the fundamentals, plus you had faith in yourself and in the project. It's paid off! You're amazing!"

"Couldn't have done it without you!" exclaimed Garry. "You're incredible, Joan! I'm heading home to tell Susan and the kids. This kind of story can't wait 'til 5!"

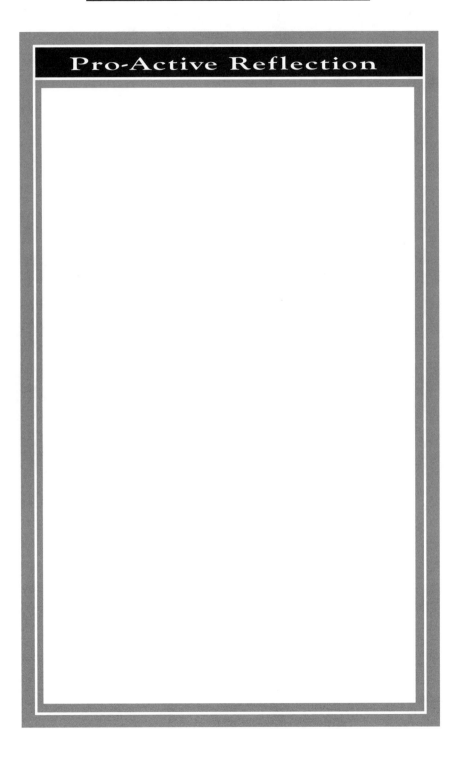

Pro-Active Reflection

CHAPTER 15

The Seeds of Success

"Garry's Teachable Moment"

*H*ad you previously thought of your successes in life as results for following patterns that allowed you to reap *the harvest* of your efforts? That is precisely what Sages understand.

In the previous chapter, we discussed *the harvest* and the patterns that needed to be implemented in order to reap its benefits. Sage individuals understand that in order to achieve consistent successes, they must be responsible not only for knowing the necessary patterns, but also for ensuring that they are followed.

Imagine how different your approach to life would be if you knew that every action you took was part of a pattern and would lead to an inevitable harvest. You would undoubtedly begin to search out the patterns that govern the successes you seek – right? And you would most certainly execute them precisely in the order required, for your *bountiful harvest* to become a reality.

In our story, Garry was doing just that. He was an entrepreneur like many of you – one who knew, as you do, that he was fully responsible for orchestrating the successes he wanted in his life. Past experience had shown him that he already knew about and applied some of the components needed in the pattern for success, but not all of them.

He also did not completely understand the importance of applying them in an orderly fashion in order to achieve the desired result. When he experienced the incredible frustration associated with *fumbling the ball*, he did what most people do when they're unaware of the laws and patterns required for success – he panicked. Fortunately, his sage friend stepped in and coached him back *into the game* – this time armed with *the plays* necessary to *score the touchdown*.

That's why you're reading this book. Like Garry, you want to know what the components for success are, as well as how to apply them to achieve the greater levels of success you desire.

Garry's sage friend reinforced the need to both understand and apply the same foundations you have learned about thus far. These are givens in the pattern for success.

They all form the basis for the *resulting* foundation of
The Harvest

This foundation of the harvest partially satisfies our *fundamental need* for fulfillment.

A harvest is the natural result when the *seeds* of the previous foundations are properly *planted, nurtured* and applied together.

In Garry's past experience, the interrelationship among the foundations couldn't exist as some of them were missing. He wasn't able to organize effectively because he wasn't even sure what he was organizing – he hadn't done his homework. His purpose wasn't totally clear in his mind. He also didn't understand that opposition is a necessary component of balance – instead of using it to his advantage, he allowed it to defeat him. However, the second time around, he had all of the pieces and could integrate them appropriately; and he achieved his goal.

Perhaps you, too, have found yourself in similar situations. You have already achieved a certain level of success, but you know that it could be much greater with the right *tools* working together at the right time.

Individually, the foundations have merit, but when combined in the proper order with the other required foundations, they are empowering. Appropriate use of these foundations depends a great deal on your understanding of the attitude that is related to the foundation of the harvest –

"You reap what you sow."

How could this attitude affect *the harvest* you are currently pursuing?

There is empowerment that comes with this attitude. Because you understand how to apply the *FaithSkills* through the foundations, you carefully choose the patterns that must be followed to achieve your goals. You know that you are in charge of seeing that they are successfully implemented, so you don't pass this responsibility to someone else.

Garry followed the same principles. He had his plan – he knew exactly what had to be done, as well as when and how it had to be done; he could proceed without guesswork or hesitancy. This knowledge provided an incredible boost to his self-esteem.

As a Sage – a smart individual – you also understand, as Garry did, that if you don't *plant the seeds* and nurture them, you can't expect the same harvest as one who does. You cannot leave anything to chance.

As you work on mastering this foundation, the benefits will become apparent.

Ponder This

Tired of Trying?

Do you now see how easily one can become frustrated and tired of trying to achieve success when they don't have a sage perspective about laws and agency? No wonder so many surrender to the terrible state of being victims – they give up and let life act upon them. Then of course there are those who try to *outsmart* the laws of success and wonder why they always seem to be on the wrong end of the stick.

Permanent success. It's real and cannot be manipulated, it can only be orchestrated when you exercise your agency, valiantly, to obey the laws that predicate the successes you desire. Learn and master those laws and you will eminently succeed. Keep the faith!

Rene Says

As a parent, salesperson, business owner/operator, I have always found it easier to relate to and communicate with people when I acknowledge their *inward* fundamental needs for acceptance, knowledge and harmony. As I accept them for the powerful and precious spirits that they are, I listen intently to what their words and actions speak. I can then ask thought-provoking questions to clarify what they perceive to be their purpose, then devote myself to mirroring it in constructive ways. This process begins to build a state of harmony. By doing this, I can often educate that person by giving them a point of reference so they can determine if what they think they want is actually what they want. Or,

Continued next page...

• You will learn to think before you act.

• If something goes wrong, you will be able to carefully analyze your plans to determine where *the holes* were, so you can redirect the collective effort accordingly.

• You will be composed under pressure because you know that you have the keys to success and understand how to use them. Others will look to you for help because they know your levelheaded approach will yield results.

• You will have a level of confidence that is refreshing; you will not be easily discouraged in any aspect of your life because you know that there are always answers once you discover the governing patterns of any given situation.

As an evolving sage individual, Garry learned to adopt these behaviors. Although he started to panic when he remembered the three pages of unfinished data, he reminded himself that he was now sage about such things – he didn't need to *lose it* – he needed to slow down and reflect on his options. When he was composed and thinking logically, instead of emotionally, he realized that he had an important team member in Joan. She not only respected The Essential Foundations he had taught her, but also applied them. He knew too that he had earned her loyalty because of his own application of the skills that support these foundations.

Garry also practiced the *FaithSkill* of **Cultivation**, the related talent for the foundation of the harvest.

Cultivation invites a *we* approach to life – one that is oriented towards the greater good. It is always evidenced in a team-building approach when dealing with people. This sounds much like *stewarding*, doesn't it? Both influence our consideration for, and our treatment of, other people.

Garry had a committed, loyal team member in Joan. This didn't occur by chance. Over the years, he had diligently cultivated this mutually beneficial relationship. As a result, both of them had learned to value each other's input and expertise. Garry knew too that he could rely on her loyalty, otherwise he would not have trusted her with such an important assignment.

Joan had also learned that she could trust Garry to look out for her interests as well as his own, so she was willing to inconvenience herself for the common good. Although he promised her a bonus for her efforts, she was more concerned

Rene Says

I can verify that their actions are producing the results they desire. This is a constructive, qualifying process for them, but also for me, in that I am educating and qualifying myself so that I can cooperate with their cause and/ or fulfill their needs in order to start building solid relationships with them. It's often referred to as Total Honest Communication. If done authentically, the spirits of others will both recognize that authenticity and sense a stability that both of you seek and need. Objections or issues then come out; you become empowered by that person. Why? Because you deal with the issues with genuine, authentic actions that the other person can similarly respond to. You empower one another to get what you both want – fulfillment, or success!

Focus Box

My thoughts...

about remaining on the team; she knew that she was part of a winning group and wanted to stay there.

As a Sage, Garry did not reserve his team-building approach only for work. He knew that Sages are constant in their behaviors, thus, he used it in all aspects of his life – including in his family.

He shared his past learning experiences and feelings with them so they could not only understand his confidence in the success of his current project, but also feel part of the winning team. They were then willing to support his plans – even another out-of-town trip – because they knew it would ultimately provide benefits for the whole family.

Do you recognize benefits for yourself if you implement the skill of cultivation? How would its use in a past situation have yielded greater results than you experienced at that time?

Mastering the skill of cultivation will lead to the development of **Charity** – the seventh of the fundamental *virtues*.

Garry demonstrated this virtue as his sage mentor had taught him. He was thrilled with his achievement, but didn't forget those who helped him attain it.

Garry not only acknowledged and praised Joan for her work, he promised her a bonus for her efforts. He also assured her that she'd remain on the team – the greatest compliment he could have paid her.

He then rushed home to share the great news with his family, knowing that they too had made sacrifices to ensure the success of the project.

Sages strive to exemplify this virtue of charity regardless of the situations in which they find themselves. They understand that this is the virtue to which the six previous virtues have led – it is the culminating and all-encompassing one – one they will continue to develop for the rest of their lives.

You've likely had experiences that have proven these concepts to be true.

Think about it

Is it right to expect fire in the fireplace without first putting in the logs? No! That's what cultivation is all about – making sure there are trees planted so you have logs to burn, today and tomorrow!

As you subscribe to the foundation of *the harvest*, you will not only orchestrate your successes according to a specific pattern, but you'll be able to claim responsibility for them as they occur.

You will also attract success in many ways as you implement all of the foundations in the proper form and order – people, events, even *coincidences*, will come your way. Are these *chance* occurrences? No. Sages know that they are the result of understanding and applying the rock solid Essential Foundations you've learned about in this book.

We are delighted that you have come so far! We hope that you are practicing the new skills you are learning – that's the only way to assimilate them.

The following chapter discusses the *governing* foundation of *Commitment*. Obviously, you *know* of this foundation – without it, you would not have stayed with us to this point.

Pro-Active Reflection

CHAPTER

16

The Best Legacy

I drove slowly down the highway, paying as little attention to the road as I dared. My mind was a thousand miles away. The circumstances of our trip had that sort of effect on both Randy and I. We were in deep and joyful thoughts. Our friend – our colleague – had passed on. We were on our way to his memorial service.

Phil had been a marvelous individual. I smiled as I thought of the many times we had joked and laughed together. He had an incredible sense of humor. He was always upbeat, regardless of the circumstances; he saw the sunny side of everything. I knew I was a better man for having known him.

Randy interrupted my thoughts. We chatted about the good times and exchanged our favorite memories of Phil. Then silence. We drove for miles with this pattern – talk, then quiet reflection.

Suddenly, Randy turned towards me and said, "No matter how you look at it, Phil was one guy you could always count on. His word was solid – whenever he said he was going to do something, you knew it was as good as done."

"You're absolutely right," I replied. "You've totally summed up the greatest compliment that could be paid to Phil. I can't begin to count the number of times he came through for his family and many friends – people like you and me."

He had always demonstrated tremendous fortitude by sticking to his word, often at the expense of his own personal gain. He was the perfect example of a man who exemplified integrity, faithfulness and loyalty. I couldn't help but wonder if I could ever be viewed in the same light.

As I reflected on the legacy he'd left behind, I was overwhelmed with a deep feeling of appreciation for the influence he'd had in our lives. Yes, it was a feeling I'd had many a time during our friendship. Life was genuinely better for all of us because of his example.

It was no wonder that he was such a success, both as a parent and a leader in business. He wasn't a millionaire in the financial sense, but he was in terms of the things that really mattered – family, friends, principles, health, and especially, happiness.

The ideal mentor, Phil exemplified what was important in life. Now, don't get me wrong – he was a business success too, but never flaunted that or anything else – he had too much respect for us – his friends.

It was amazing. I suddenly remembered a business convention I'd attended with Phil. In the afternoon between seminars, he and I were sitting in the hotel lobby relaxing. We suddenly found ourselves surrounded with fellow conventioneers, all past employees of Phil's. Many had gone on to own their own businesses or manage the businesses of his direct competitors.

They kibitzed and joked together like the old friends they were. Phil seemed to genuinely enjoy their company. Later, he bragged to me, with great pride, about the successes that each of them had achieved.

I was stunned that he would say that. I even remember his exact words to me, because I couldn't believe that someone would think that way. He said: "They were great students. They make me proud. Evidently, I must have taught them something right, or they couldn't have gone on to what they're doing now."

It was at that moment that I recognized Phil for the Sage he was. His attitude inspired me to always look at the positive side of things, for as he said, "You've got to make lemonade out of the lemons or you'll end up like the rest of them – a sourpuss."

Yes. We were all better off for having known Phil. I smiled at the thought of his firm handshake. Even though we'd been friends for a long time, Phil loved to greet me and all of his friends with a handshake. It demonstrated his genuine pleasure to see us again.

Internationally recognized for excellence in his industry, Phil was much more than the *run of the mill* local franchise operator everyone thought he was. He was astute, careful, caring and honest, but especially, he was committed. Everyone who worked with him knew without a doubt that they could have total faith in his word. His passion for commitment made him a solid pillar for all of us to emulate.

I remembered another occasion when his example deeply touched me. I was at one of his stores and overheard him talking with his manager.

"Son, I know that you're afraid to commit to hitting these new targets. It's going to mean that some serious changes will need to take place here. But I can promise you that true commitment on your part will bring about immense changes in your life – changes that will make you a better man. That's what commitment does to us. It makes us better and stronger than if we'd never mustered up the courage to try."

I never told Phil how that mentoring moment had affected me. Until then, I'd never seen any personal benefit in making a commitment to someone else. From that moment on, however, I had a different perspective about it. I recognized that Phil was right – it was a growing opportunity, not just another demand on my time.

I suddenly realized we'd traveled 50 miles and not spoken a word. Both Randy and I were lost in thought. We weren't sad, just reflective.

I looked over at him and saw him smirking. His eye caught mine. He smiled and said, "You know, Phil had this uncanny ability to teach you something when you didn't know you were being taught. Do you know what I mean?"

"I sure do. He called those teachable moments."

"Yeah. That's right. I remember when he taught me about how he kept his word."

"Really? What did he tell you?"

"Well, he didn't tell me directly, but indirectly, he taught me and everyone else that was in his store that day. Phil's son was mopping the floor, but with a very casual, uncaring attitude. He was taking a long time and not doing a very thorough job. Phil came in, and without saying a word, watched him for awhile. He then walked over to his son, put his arm around his shoulders and said, "If you're as casual about life as you are casual about mopping the floor, you'll end up being a casualty of life."

"Everyone in the showroom, including his son, had a chuckle about his little proverb. Phil, however, wasn't trying to be funny. He spun around, and looked his son right in the eye."

"Son, where do you think I'd be if I committed myself to my business like you've committed to mopping the floor? Pretty scary thought, isn't it? Remember: when I ask you to commit yourself, I expect the same from you as I do from myself. I want your heart, might and mind – nothing less. Otherwise, your word is nothing more than idle talk."

"We were all impressed. We knew that he lived this belief. Phil was a man of his word; his word was as good as cash in the bank."

I could tell that Randy was touched as he rehearsed the story to me. Phil's legacy was immense and far-reaching.

He had demonstrated to us that the fundamentals of success need not be formed by the standards of the world, but rather by what he often referred to as his Essential Foundations. Over the years, he had casually mentioned them to me, but I hadn't paid much attention before now.

I'd wondered earlier if I could ever be worthy of the kind of honor that Phil had received. If using those Essential Foundations could do that for me, it was time I took out those papers he'd given me years ago and tried them out.

How about that Phil? Even in death, you still have a profound influence over me. Because of you, there's a good possibility that I can become more like you – I'd like nothing better! Thanks, Phil, for the legacy!

194

Pro-Active Reflection

CHAPTER

17

Mirror, Mirror On The Wall

"Our Teachable Moment"

A legacy is defined as something handed down from a predecessor or ancestor. It is a positive investment in a future generation – one that can provide a foundation for unlimited successes. A legacy can include such tangible things as property or money, or intangibles like honesty, faith or integrity.

In the previous chapter, we focused on the legacy of commitment. In and of itself, it would be considered intangible, yet its results are clearly observable.

Commitment satisfies our *fundamental need* for **fulfillment**

It must play an integral part in anyone's plans for success.

Your success thus far has shown that you understand the importance of this foundation and its implementation in your activities, just as Phil did. This understanding may have come about through your own past experiences or by observing the actions of others.

In our story or parable, both Randy and his friend had learned much from watching their sage friend, Phil. They had likely learned something about commitment in their own experiences in business, but observing Phil led them to clarify and solidify their adoption of this important foundation.

Phil learned about the Essential Foundations one segment at a time, just as you are doing. It was obvious from his actions and from the comments made about him that he knew how to organize himself and his life's circumstances to achieve his purposes. He wasn't afraid of opposition because he understood its purpose. His quiet confidence in his own abilities encouraged the development of such *FaithSkills* talents as devotion, humility, discipline, and authenticity. Other people recognized his influence as a great leader

Rene Says

Hope, faith and Charity are the pure languages of love. Hope is the language of the spirit. It comes from within and is always the seed of love. We hope for things for people we care for, and thus often express our spirit's will in the form of wishes. You then submit your physical self by exercising faith in the cause or person that you have expressed hope for by allowing your spirit's will to act upon your physical being. This results in some kind of physical action that expresses your love or faith – you donate, you listen, you phone, and so on. When you exercise charity – the supreme act of love – you give of your entire self by giving of your time. You see, charity is

Continued next page...

and wanted to emulate his amazing example, particularly Randy's friend. He recognized that Phil's adherence to the Essential Foundations helped to determine who he was – a faithful, committed man.

Commitment is the essence of integrity. When it is rooted in your spirit, it touches you and can change you instantly, not just for a few days or months, but for life. As Phil pointed out to his manager, it will make you a stronger, better person.

Commitment, or the lack of it, has affected everyone at one time or another. Reflect for a moment on an experience in your life when commitment was not exercised. What happened? Wasn't your spirit *touched* by the negative result? How would it have been different if you and/or your team members had been more committed?

From such experiences, Sages have learned about the attitude that is built upon the foundation of commitment. It is that:

"You Can Only Fully Commit through Faith."

To think of commitment in any other terms is to put on blinders.

Knowing this, Sages focus on

200

coaching their team members to become more knowledgeable, more involved in decision-making, and more responsible, in order to promote faithfulness to the cause. Total, honest two-way communication is an important part of this process, as is being an example of the type of faithful, committed behavior that is desired.

Being faithful means giving *all* of yourself – your spirit, mind and body. When your spirit is empowered to act upon your body, your commitment is pure. This is faith.

Are you an example of a committed leader? Is it evident to your team? If not, changes need to happen – right?

In our story, Phil provided many examples of his own level of commitment. But, he also knew how important it was to anyone who was striving for success, so he was not afraid to encourage his team members to apply this foundation for their own development, not just for the sake of his business. Consider his manager and his son.

The young manager was afraid to commit to reaching the new targets. Why? Was he afraid he couldn't do it? Was he unwilling to make the necessary changes in himself or his surroundings because he was comfortable where he was and didn't want to stretch?

Rene Says

the actual *walking the talk* of giving. That's what love is – giving. When we are charitable, we do more than sign a check or drop coins into the Salvation Army kettle. We offer our entire selves – spirit, mind and body – or in other words, our time. Remember that time is a measurement made for man by man. It only occurs when all three dimensions of our being exist. If there is no spirit, there is no need for time. If no mind, time is totally irrelevant. No body, time is totally unnecessary. Nothing is greater than giving of your time to a person or cause, because when you do, you're giving all of yourself. That's why Charity is pure love. You are totally accepting because you're totally giving.

Focus Box

My thoughts...

Phil tried to help him understand that making commitments would provide great personal benefits – he could satisfy the *what's in it for me* question as well as help the company.

His son was doing the job of mopping the floor, but had little interest in doing it well – he wasn't at all committed to it, likely because he didn't feel it was important.

Phil tried to help him understand that it's important to commit to doing any task well, anytime, anywhere – not just when you feel like it or see it as necessary.

Neither Phil's manager nor his son understood how to be faithful to the tasks at hand, thus they could not truly commit to them, or appreciate the benefits of doing so.

Remember that in order to truly commit, the intelligence must be involved as well as the spirit. The spirit then exerts its will upon the body. Without a full commitment of the spirit, Sages know that one is quick to abandon the cause.

Reflect on a time when someone fell through on his or her commitment to you. How did you feel? Now consider a time when someone came through for you. How did you feel then? How important is it to you to be able to count on someone's word? Note your thoughts in the box to the left.

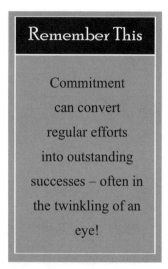

Remember This

Commitment can convert regular efforts into outstanding successes – often in the twinkling of an eye!

Obviously, your feelings would be different in each situation. Do you see that when the spirit is not committed, neither is the body. Thus the cause is dropped?

All of the Essential Foundations require the active participation of the spirit in order to become a permanent part of one's life and growth process.

The foundation of Commitment is the natural culmination of all previous foundations. Much as a special lid can convert a pot into a powerful pressure cooker, so can commitment affect the Essential Foundations and empower them to become the incredible success *enablers* in your life that they were intended to be.

Now lets examine the *heat* for that pressure cooker – **Faithfulness** – the *FaithSkill* associated with commitment.

Phil knew how to be faithful to his goals because he had learned how to exercise faith in himself by diligently applying the previous *FaithSkills*, through the Essential Foundations, in order to meet his *fundamental needs.* You can likely think of many examples from the story, but here are a few for you to consider. When facing opposition, in terms of the reluctance of his manager to strive to achieve new targets, Phil was fearless in explaining the benefits of change and commitment. He was authentic. He acted the same regardless of the circumstances or people involved. People recognized that what they saw was who he really was. He was also comfortable with who he was and what he had accomplished, so he didn't need to flaunt his successes to others, nor did he resent it when his trainees went on to become successful. Phil understood the patterns required for

Ponder This

It's What We All Want!

A legacy is what every human being strives to create in his or her lifetime. No matter which way you look at it, we still want attention even after we're gone. That's what a legacy is – attention after we're gone.

The *FaithSkills* Personal Operating System can assure you of a Royal Legacy – one that will be cherished by your posterity for generations after your departure, even into eternity. Why? Because *FaithSkills* touch the lives of everyone you meet – they are actions of the spirit.

You not only fulfill your own *fundamental needs*, you help others fulfill theirs as well. It's a life of service that creates service. It's Eternal.

success and adapted them to create his own *FaithSkills* operating system – one that would lead to the accomplishments that he defined as *success:* faithful commitment to family, friends, business and self.

Do you feel that your team members are faithful to your cause? Why or why not? Are you faithful to it? Are you faithful to your team? You may have just found a solution!

There's a great synergy that happens when everyone is faithful to the task at hand. This combination of faithful energies can indeed make the efforts of three seem like the work of ten. The results are always enormous because the efforts of each individual are quantified by the others.

The *virtue* of **Charity** evolves from the FaithSkill of faithfulness.

Phil was a charitable man. He cared about other people with a depth that many would have considered unusual, perhaps even unnecessary. He was more concerned about others than he was about himself. Consider these examples; he was quick to acknowledge the accomplishments of his former employees: he never flaunted his successes to those around him; he never took advantage of people.

You see, Phil had satisfied his spirit's

fundamental need for fulfillment through the results of his charitable actions. He didn't need the artificial fulfillment that many gain at the expense of others. He was complete; others knew it and benefited from it.

The charitable actions of such Sages leave indelible impressions on other people. Why? Because they are offered without conditions or ulterior motives.

People are drawn to these Sages in any environment and gladly support them in leadership positions because they are trustworthy and wise in the ways of success.

Has your definition of charity changed as a result of your new knowledge?

How can this virtue influence and benefit you and those around you?

Food for thought isn't it? It's moments like these that quantify your progress. Take time to fully cultivate them and grow from the inside out like never before.

Pro-Active Reflection

CHAPTER

18

Be A Permanent Success

"Our Summary Sage Reflection"

*W*e hope this last Sage Reflection will help to clarify any questions or concerns you might have.

You first exercised your agency to read this book in order to convert intelligence, which you possess, into new knowledge. You were then invited to reflect on this new knowledge and awaken your spirit, to discern its truth and determine its value to you in this life.

If you did this, you positioned yourself to enjoy your own revelatory experience – to be *moved* or *touched*, if you will, in that, you intellectually verified and spiritually certified that what you converted, or discovered, was indeed true and valuable to you.

Whenever a man or woman is *moved* in this way, great and marvelous works can occur; works that are permanent and positive, the kind that can literally *move the mountains of our lives*.

That's what *permanent success* is – a state of being that is attained and maintained by living a life that is spirit driven, one that *moves* you to progress from one success to another, day in and day out.

For Sages, every experience is a success, regardless of the circumstances. It is clearly understood that every experience is a revealing experience because we can discover and learn who we really are through the actions of our lives.

The one and only skill that facilitates the creation of this *state of being* is faith. Faith is all about *moving* people; it is the projection of our spirit's hope into this physical world.

There are varying degrees of faith. The first is having faith in ourselves, the second, faith in others, and the third and greatest degree, having faith in Deity, whatever you perceive that to be.

All things in this world evolve or grow; faith is no different. That's why it is absolutely impossible to think that we can effectively exercise the second and third degrees of faith if we can't even exercise the first.

By exercising faith in yourself, you acknowledge your *spirit* and allow it to be involved in every action of your day. You can then start the awesome experience of *mining* the limitless well of intelligence that you already possess.

I call this *the spiral of faith*. As a building force, your basic cycle of exercising faith in yourself moves you forward through the virtues you develop. As you do, you can begin to effectively and confidently exercise faith at the second and third levels.

This book is all about dealing with the foundations of this so deeply-misunderstood skill of faith – practical faith. I hope you can now see how it relates to *permanent success* – the two are synonymous. However, without an understanding of faith, one must think of *permanent success* as mere wishful thinking.

I am certain that that's what many of you thought when you picked up this book: *permanent success? Nothing's permanent in this life.* You're right, if you think of *permanence* in terms of the physical things of this world. However, think of it in terms of the spirit. *Permanence* then becomes a reality because once your spirit is *touched*, permanent changes occur.

As we briefly review the stories, please note how this principle applies. Let's begin with the story of Cameron.

Not only had his self-esteem taken a beating, but he thought he was facing an unsolvable problem. However, his mother knew that by guiding him to an understanding of the foundations of **organization**, **order** and **purpose**, both issues would be resolved.

Through the *FaithSkill* of **Stewardship,** Angela guided Cameron to recognize his need for the foundation of Organization. Water was the perfect teaching tool for illustrating her point.

Angela then impressed upon him the need for the *FaithSkill* of **Obedience** so that he could appreciate the Essential Foundation of

Order. Once Cameron understood this, he was prepared to begin to fill his need for **Acceptance.**

Angela's use of the *FaithSkill* of **Devotion** empowered her to help Cameron understand why he needed math in his life and how it could benefit him. This information satisfied Cameron's *fundamental need* for **Knowledge.**

Thus, instead of turning into an unpleasant lecture experience, the discussion became a growth experience for Cameron, as well as a bonding time for him and his mother. The spirit's needs were heard and fulfilled through an understanding of the Essential Foundations and associated *FaithSkills*: outward actions, such as discussion, directed questioning, and relating tangible items (water) to intangible subjects (math), fulfilled the inward, spiritual needs for acceptance and knowledge, thus the learning became permanent in his mind so he could apply the principles in future situations.

Cindy and James also learned about satisfying needs. Circumstances that could have supplied bricks for the house of divorce turned out to be memorable bonding experiences that acted as mortar in the palace of a happy marriage.

Cindy nurtured James to see his weaknesses by using the *FaithSkills* of **Cooperation** and **Fearlessness** to clarify his understanding of the Essential Foundations of **Balance** and **Opposition**. She could have been selfish in exposing these foundations, using them as weapons against James with the intention of making him feel foolish. Instead, she selflessly used the teaching moments resulting from the sunburn experience to satisfy both her own and her husband's *fundamental need* for **Harmony**. She also expanded on Ken's discussion of opposition and why it is necessary for achieving balance.

We then experienced the choice opportunity of hearing a Sage, William (Bill) Anderson, use the *FaithSkills* of **Reflection** and **Humility** to share pearls of wisdom about the benefits of another *FaithSkill* – that of **Discipline**. Without this talent, self-fulfillment, or success, would have been impossible.

Bill also revealed to us that the greatest success we can ever have is to know who we really are – to know our **Identity** – an **Intelligence** formed into a **Spirit** that presently occupies a **Body**. Once we know this, we are able to effectively fulfill our *fundamental needs* through the actions of this life, as William so effectively demonstrated.

Without this understanding, we don't really satisfy our needs – we only think we do when we become entrapped in the never-ending circle of materialism which forms this physical life sphere we presently occupy. William demonstrated that fulfilling our spirit's *fundamental needs* yields bountiful fruits of success.

Does this understanding give you a new perspective regarding the accumulation of this life's *toys*?

We then met Cyrus and Robert, our cranberry experts – two sincere individuals with two different strategies and styles for solving the same problem. We can all relate to that. It translates to *trying to get the most out of life.*

Cyrus used his **Agency** to determine the best **Action** to take in making his property productive. His neighbor, Robert, was highly impressed with this impact and wanted to know how to experience similar results.

Robert demonstrated **Humility**, which enabled Cyrus to **Honestly** explain to him his understanding of the *governing* laws of his circumstances. Cyrus then used the *FaithSkills* of **Valiance** and **Authenticity** to have a profound impact upon his circumstances, rather than have them act upon him.

This new understanding allowed Robert to satisfy his *fundamental needs* for **Direction** and **Empowerment**. He now had a new direction – Humility had moved him forward to gain what he knew he deserved – Success.

It was after this story that we introduced you to Garry. He had already worn a path on a journey of learning, but thanks to his sage mentor, he was steered to the *FaithSkill* of **Reflection**.

We witnessed him trying to apply his understandings of the Essential Foundations and *FaithSkills* to a new situation. He didn't do it perfectly – none of us would – but he didn't give up.

We watched him catch himself as he realized he was missing a key step on his ladder of success – the basic *FaithSkill* of **Reflection**. It was then that he remembered the valuable ally he had in Joan. Through use of the *FaithSkill* of **Cultivation**, he had encouraged her loyalty over a period of time and knew that he could count on her.

Gary wasn't embarrassed by his past failed attempts at achieving success – he thought of them as learning experiences and shared them with his family, so they too could learn. By doing so, he gained the strength that comes from Humility.

He could then activate the Essential Foundation of **The Law of The Harvest** to satisfy a portion of his *fundamental need* for Fulfillment.

From this platform, we introduced you to the culminating story of *The Best Legacy*. It was Phil's story that demonstrated how a *FaithSkills* based life could be one of permanent successes. His profound understanding of the *FaithSkill* of **Faithfulness** empowered him to fully commit himself to what he *knew*, through his spirit, was true. He also understood that The Essential Foundation of *Commitment* could completely and permanently satisfy his *fundamental need* for *Fulfillment,* or in other words – Success. The result? An incredible legacy.

Don't many of us wish to leave a similar, honorable legacy?

We mentioned earlier that in order for you to think of success as *permanent*, you need to consider it in terms of the spirit. Reflect for a moment on how one or more of the characters in each story exercised practical faith – faith in themselves – because they recognized the influence of the spirit in their lives – their actions *felt right*.

Hopefully, the range of situations shown in the stories gives you an idea of the myriad of different ways that practical faith can be applied to lead to success. However, there may be some of you that are thinking, *so how can all of this help me in my daily activities?*

Let's translate this information into practical terms.

Let's say you're in a leadership position – you own a business. You have 5 employees. They do their work, but they don't have any sense of *team spirit*, nor do they feel any particular loyalty to you or your cause.

Through reflection on the situation, you wonder if that's because they don't feel like they belong in your workplace, nor do they understand exactly what you're trying to accomplish with your business, or what role they play in it.

So, what have you accomplished so far? You've determined that two of the *fundamental needs*, namely acceptance, or belonging, as well as knowledge, are not being met. You know that you need to use the Essential Foundations of organization, order and purpose to meet these needs.

What will you organize? Work stations? Tasks? Staff meetings? Flow of paperwork? Reporting system? People?

In what order will you organize the items needing attention? Will you prioritize in terms of time? Will the staff meeting come first? Will you rearrange the work stations?

What do you want to accomplish with your organization and order – in other words, what is your purpose? What knowledge do you want to share? How can you best do this?

As you organize the important items, and put them into an order, you'll want to do it with consideration for the common good, so you'll encourage your employees to ask questions and offer suggestions, both of which foster a greater sense of belonging and team spirit. You'll use a *coaching* style, rather than a preaching or dictatorial approach as you work with them. This is the essence of the skill of stewardship, the skill that relates to the Essential Foundation of organization.

With this approach, employees will be more willing to

follow or conform to the established order, not only because they've had some input into the plan, but also because they understand the reasons for it and how it can benefit them as a group. This knowledge then paves the way for their devotion to the cause.

Don't forget that you're also developing virtues as you implement the foundations. When you have to sit down and determine what needs to be organized and how, you sharpen your ability to discern – to figure out what's important and what isn't; what will influence and what won't; who can do a certain task and who can't, and so on. You then become more *self-reliant* because you have faith in yourself and your knowledge of the game plan for success.

I'm sure that what we've just discussed is familiar to you. You've likely used some of these foundations before. You've probably also developed several of the skills and virtues; you see, you've already started your success building process!

This world we live in is a point of intersection – a point of transition – where spiritual and physical meet. The results of this life are determined by which side dominates – the physical or the spiritual – as is the new form that is created through the melding of these two dimensions.

We're here to fulfill a progressive and permanent cycle of learning: one where we learn how to give the spirit power over the physical in order to achieve the permanent successes we desire.

A state of *permanent success* starts here, in this life you're living today. And it can only occur through the use of practical faith, or *FaithSkills*.

The next chapter will provide a detailed explanation of *FaithSkills* and how their use can empower you to achieve the state of being known as *permanent success*.

Pro-Active Reflection

CHAPTER

19

FaithSkills

"It was the best of times, it was the worst of times."

Now, more than ever, does this classic statement by Charles Dickens gain validity in describing the status of the world and the circumstances in which we live.

"Why?" you ask. "Capacity is why."

Just as reading the preceding chapters of this book has prepared you for growth, or change, by increasing your capacity to learn the basics of the FaithSkills Personal Operating System, so has the corruption of society increased the capacity of mankind to foolishly and effectively eliminate itself from the progressive cycle of this world.

How is this happening?

We are currently experiencing the *best of times* in terms of the knowledge explosion that makes life more fast-paced, interesting, exciting and convenient. Yet, the *worst of times* presents its ugliness in the form of corruption, exploitation, subversion and tyranny, to name just a few.

And the result of such negativity? We have little or no confidence in others, particularly in those who lead our countries – it has been shattered.

Despite the enormous freedom we have to choose, or place our trust and faith in these leaders, the more we seem to become trapped by their abuse of the power we've given them.

Did you notice the irony here? It seems that the more freedom we gain, the more willing we are to turn to others for direction, which effectively robs us of the freedom we have. Then we become increasingly frustrated because of the tremendous gap between what we perceive should happen and what actually happens.

How does this affect us personally in the area of self-esteem? We lose the ability to believe in ourselves and our abilities; in other

Rene Says

Contrary to a common misunderstanding, change does not take time – it's the preparation for change, which is always required in order for it to occur, that takes time. This misunderstanding often causes many to give up on the process of change, or worse yet, deny when it occurs. You see, many people may unknowingly be living a life that prepares them for the enormous changes they may suddenly seek to orchestrate. Because they've unconsciously done the *homework – bam* – they occur. It's possible! I have seen it countless times. However, there are others who are so far away from where they want to go that they refute the need for preparation and never

Continued next page...

words, we lose faith in ourselves. A sad situation when considering that this is the *psychosaic age*, or age of the mind as described by Earl Nightingale, and should provide many opportunities for learning that would enhance our belief in ourselves, not destroy it.

To further complicate matters, we've allowed our minds to overshadow our spirits and downplay their influence in our lives. Now, however, is the time to meld the physical, intellectual and spiritual parts of our lives in order to achieve our goals. All three parts of our beings must be involved in order to achieve the successes we desire. We are then prepared to *be right*, or in other words, to live a spiritually based life, instead of living a *do right* – physically based life – or a *think right* – intellectually based life.

That's why I've written this book and developed the *FaithSkills* pattern – to help prepare you for the process of change that is required to live a *be right* kind of life. You will need to recognize the interrelationship between faith in self, *FaithSkills*, and permanent success in order to accomplish this.

Hopefully, what you have learned so far has empowered you to fill your own *fundamental needs* as well as satisfy the *fundamental needs* of others. This is the

220

way of life, or *state of being* known as *permanent success*.

You have already learned a lot about the skills set known as *FaithSkills*. You have seen in the stories how they can be applied in real life situations to help achieve success.

This is my intention – to guide you in acquiring the practical, not theoretical, keys to success.

I have learned first hand, from my own experience, as well as through the mentoring and studying of many other successful individuals, that faith is a practical skill. I can assure you that the sooner one becomes empowered to exercise it, the sooner one begins to create enduring, lasting successes.

Now that you know what *FaithSkills* are, you are ready to learn how to form them. You are also prepared to learn about the *abilities* that can evolve into the *skills* that precede the development of these *FaithSkills talents*. Each of these is part of a different level of awareness. Each level requires a different focus for your thinking. These focuses are drawn from the three parts of our being that identify who we are, namely, the intelligence, spirit and body. In order to achieve enduring successes, our ultimate goal is to adopt a spirit based, spirit driven, focus, which is developed through the

Rene Says

make the changes stick. They may make those needed to accommodate the requirements, but do they walk the talk? Often not! Permanent positive changes occur when the spirit is touched; they come from the inside out. That's why they're permanent. *Think about it.* Isn't that what happens when the smoker quits after he's lost a loved one to lung cancer? Whenever the spirit's touched, permanent positive changes occur in the twinkling on an eye. So, don't get down on yourself when things don't happen as quickly or solidly as you've anticipated. Look at how you're preparing to make those changes and make them from the inside out. You'll be amazed at the capacity and patience of your inner being.

Think about it

Physically based life – fuelled by necessity to take care of immediate physical needs.

Intellectually based life – fuelled by the mind to satisfy individual curiosity.

Spiritually based life – satisfies our *fundamental needs*, the needs of our spirit and when developed are for the greater good.

talents known as *FaithSkills*.

Most of us are not there yet. We are at various stages in the 3 areas, in that we may have adopted some of the *abilities* that form the physical or *body* focus, some that fall under the *skills* that form the intelligence or *mind* focus, while still others may be part of the *talents* that form the *spiritual* focus. Each of the three areas form their own Personal Operating Systems, thus you may choose to live your life according to a physically based system, an intellectually based system, or a spiritually based system. However, be aware that it is the spiritually based system of *FaithSkills* that develops the enduring or lasting successes you desire. This system empowers you to not only have faith in yourself, but to allow others to exercise faith in you as you exercise faith in them.

Remember: it all starts with you. You first need to have faith in yourself before you can have it in others.

So, let's start your personal process of reclaiming the skill of faith. You will see that it is not mysterious but in fact, is a practical skill.

The process will be explained as follows. Each FaithSkill *talent* will be represented in a chart that shows the progression from an *ability* (physically based) to a *skill* (intellectually based) to the FaithSkill *talent* itself (spiritually based).

Each ability, skill, and talent are organized into a column that represents the personal operating system it supports.

Abilities in the physically based Personal Operating System (body). Skills in the intellectually based personal operating system (mind) and of course talents in the spiritually based personal operating system (spirit).

These three Personal Operating Systems are clearly identified by the use of triangles, that represent prisms, which ideally symbolize our three dimensional beings – body, mind and spirit.

Just as a prism refracts sunlight, our actions exhibit our core beliefs. Only when our actions are applied through our spirits can we produce effects that are easily viewed for all around us to see. Actions speak volumes about who we really are.

The 13 *FaithSkills* are:

- Stewardship
- Obedience
- Devotion
- Cooperation
- Fearlessness
- Reflection
- Humility
- Discipline
- Honesty
- Valiance
- Authenticity
- Cultivation
- Faithfulness

223

The *FaithSkill* of Stewardship

The Progression from Abilities to Talents:

Once you understand the Essential Foundation of *Organization,* you are able to master the physical *Ability* to be a Builder, then the intellectual *Skill* of Administration, and then, ultimately the *FaithSkill Talent* of *Stewardship*.

can become

can become

A Needs Filling
FaithSkill
TALENT

A Needs Filling
SKILL

ADMINISTRATION

A Needs Filling
ABILITY

BUILDER

The
Doorway
connects
actions to
real needs

Our
Real
Need

STEWARDSHIP

Is the talent by which we facilitate the organization of the people, elements and circumstances of the environment in which we live without taking ownership of it. We have no need to because our needs are understood to be more than physical – they are spiritual. This leads to fulfillment, which comes from the acceptance of others whose needs are being filled by our own needs-filling actions.

Once we can build it, we are capable of managing, supervising and organizing the building of what we need or want. By increasing our knowledge, we develop skills and administer the organization of things as we perceive they should be, but our satisfaction is still physically driven and never fully satisfied. Thus we need to ultimately Master the spiritually based *FaithSkill* Talent of Stewardship.

When we are physically based in our actions, we satisfy the need for acceptance by building what we physically want. Often, we confuse our physical wants with our spirit's needs. We must be able to build what we need in order to guide others to build what we need through the Skill of Administration.

O R G A N I Z A T I O N

A C C E P T A N C E

Physically Based

Intellectually Based

Spiritually Based

The
Essential
Foundation

The
Fundamental
Need

NOTE: Once you choose the physical, intellectual, or spiritual Personal Operating System you desire to live by, you must then master and maintain the ability, skill or talent of that System. Only then will you have the capacity to progress to the next needs filling ability, skill or talent within the system you've chosen to live by.

STEWARDSHIP

Stewardship is the first *FaithSkill* talent that must be eventually mastered in order for any chance of permanence to occur in your success building process. Without it, your efforts fall into the trap of ownership and become possessive; possessions are not permanent.

Remember: that's why so many claim that permanent success isn't possible; they're right, if success is viewed as a possession.

Stewards understand that they must take responsibility for the issues and the results, thus, they take control of the organization whenever necessary in order to fulfill their innate and *fundamental need* for Acceptance.

Sages become proven builders and proficient administrators because of their understanding of the Essential Foundation of Organization. They are then prepared to progress towards effective mastery of the talent of stewardship to the benefit of all who surround them.

This *we* approach to supervision, management and administration motivates all those who experience it due to the evident concern for the greater good that stewardship emulates.

The *FaithSkill* of Obedience

The Progression from Abilities to Talents:

Once you understand the Essential Foundation of *Order,* you are able to master the physical *Ability* to be a Follower, then the intellectual *Skill* of Respect, and then, ultimately, the *FaithSkill Talent* of *Obedience*.

can become

can become

A Needs Filling
FaithSkill
TALENT

A Needs Filling FaithSkill TALENT	The Doorway connects actions to real needs	Our Real Need

A Needs Filling
SKILL

RESPECT

A Needs Filling
ABILITY

FOLLOWER

OBEDIENCE

When one is spiritually driven, he or she quickly recognizes and respects the need to obey the foundation of order so that the need for acceptance can be satisfied. Only through order can one find his or her place in this life, and thus satisfy the spirit's deep *fundamental need* to belong and be accepted.

As one proficiently follows an established organization, he or she gains respect for the order of things as they are and also understands the need for order to gain acceptance. Careful analysis of circumstances empowers an individual to fully appreciate respect. He or she is then prepared to ultimately master the *FaithSkill* Talent of Obedience.

In order for individuals to physically satisfy their need for acceptance through the Foundation of Order, they must be followers of the organization and its order. Once they do, they are able to appreciate the Skill of Respect.

O R D E R

A C C E P T A N C E

Physically Based

Intellectually Based

Spiritually Based

The Essential Foundation

The Fundamental Need

NOTE: Once you choose the physical, intellectual, or spiritual Personal Operating System you desire to live by, you must then master and maintain the ability, skill or talent of that System. Only then will you have the capacity to progress to the next needs filling ability, skill or talent within the system you've chosen to live by.

OBEDIENCE

Obedience is the key to gaining complete acceptance. Only when we have been able to prove that we will respect the order of things to the point that we obey it, will we fulfill our spirit's need for acceptance. Since we innately know that everything is organized into an order, we have no trouble justifying that organization and completing it.

We automatically seek to understand the order, or procedures required, so that we may complete our natural desire to organize and create. (Think of baking a cake. If we don't organize the ingredients and follow the order given by the recipe when combining them, we may not achieve the results we could have had if we had obeyed the *rules.*)

We must also be able to actually submit our entire selves, through obedience, to the implementation and stewardship of order. As others witness your adherence to obedience, they experience it's forming skill – respect; and thus benefit from your application of this powerful *FaithSkill.* The result – more acceptance from others.

The fact is we're creatures of order, which is why we organize our physical behaviors into orderly patterns that are known as habits. Go ahead. Tell me you don't have a habit. Try putting on your shirt a different way the next time you get dressed or better yet, try to dry yourself differently after you've taken a shower. Go ahead and do it for 3 days. It's almost impossible!

The *FaithSkill* of Devotion

The Progression from Abilities to Talents:

Once you understand the Essential Foundation of *Purpose,* you are able to master the physical *Ability* to be a Worker, then the intellectual *Skill* of Questioning, and then, ultimately the *FaithSkill Talent* of *Devotion.*

can become

can become

A Needs Filling ABILITY

WORKER

The ability to work effectively, physically satisfies our need to know why we're here – it fulfills the foundation of Purpose. When we're good at what we do, we especially feel a sense of purpose. We can then develop the Skill of Questioning.

Physically Based

A Needs Filling SKILL

QUESTIONING

The more effective we become at satisfying our need for knowledge in a physically based system, the more we might question the events and circumstances of our individual lives to determine what else there is. We can then ultimately master the *FaithSkill* Talent of Devotion.

Intellectually Based

A Needs Filling *FaithSkill* TALENT

DEVOTION

When we are spiritually based in our actions to satisfy the innate need for knowledge as to why we are here, we become devoted to not only discovering our purpose but also fulfilling it. Sage individuals work and question devotedly to satisfy their need to know why.

Spiritually Based

The Doorway connects actions to real needs

P U R P O S E

The Essential Foundation

Our Real Need

K N O W L E D G E

The Fundamental Need

NOTE: Once you choose the physical, intellectual, or spiritual Personal Operating System you desire to live by, you must then master and maintain the ability, skill or talent of that System. Only then will you have the capacity to progress to the next needs filling ability, skill or talent within the system you've chosen to live by.

DEVOTION

Devotion is a talent that is spiritually based. Wise individuals – Sages – know that you can only fully succeed when you become devoted to your reason for being here, which is to be capable of progression in all areas of life.

Devotion requires the submission of your entire being. Only when that occurs, will you be able to fully satisfy your spirit's *fundamental need* to gain knowledge, so you can understand why you are here at this time, in this place, with the people who surround you.

As sure as the sun rises in the east each morning, every one of us not only wants to know that we belong here and that we are accepted, but that we are fulfilling our innate purpose to gain knowledge while we are here.

As you may recall, we explained to you that we are intelligences formed into spirits having a physical experience. Our spirits know that we have all intelligence within us and that we are here to convert it into knowledge through these marvelous bodies that we reside in. Remember: the body is a vessel that manifests our spirit.

As we devote ourselves to discover our *why*, or our purpose, we gain knowledge of who we really are.

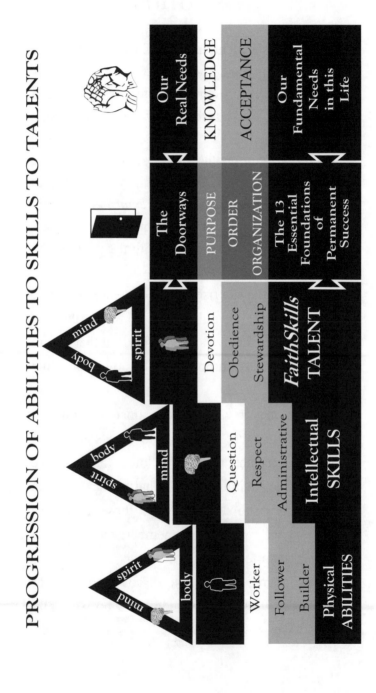

PROGRESSION OF ABILITIES TO SKILLS TO TALENTS

Our Real Needs
KNOWLEDGE
ACCEPTANCE
Our Fundamental Needs in this Life

The Doorways
PURPOSE
ORDER
ORGANIZATION
The 13 Essential Foundations of Permanent Success

Devotion
Obedience
Stewardship
FaithSkills TALENT

Question
Respect
Administrative
Intellectual SKILLS

Worker
Follower
Builder
Physical ABILITIES

mind · body · spirit

OUR PROGRESS TO DATE

In the accompanying chart, we have systematically demonstrated how you can develop the *fundamental* portions of the Essential Foundations, which are Organization, Order and Purpose. By taking your abilities and enhancing them to become skills and then *FaithSkills* talents, you can satisfy your inward *fundamental needs* for Acceptance and Knowledge.

Talents are a collection of various skills and abilities that are orchestrated from within. They effectively facilitate success that would otherwise be impossible to achieve through the use of any ability or skill individually. Once you understand how to take your physical abilities and expand them into intellectually developed skills, you will be able to recognize and facilitate their culmination into a *FaithSkills* talent.

As you can see, the adjoining chart clearly demonstrates *permanent success* does have a pattern.

Step by step we can, and should, evolve our personal methods of operating from our basic physical needs filling abilities, to our intellectually verified needs and wants, to our encompassing and totally satisfying *FaithSkills* talents which directly addresses our spirit's needs

The *FaithSkill* of Cooperation

The Progression from Abilities to Talents:

Once you understand the Essential Foundation of *Balance,* you are able to master the physical *Ability* to be a Juggler, then the intellectual *Skill* of Justifying, and then, ultimately, the *FaithSkill* *Talent* of *Cooperation*.

can become

can become

A Needs Filling
FaithSkill
TALENT

COOPERATION

Once we can physically multi-task issues and concepts and think them through, we are able to understand how important cooperation, not juggling or justifying, is to achieving balance in all aspects of our lives. Sage individuals always seek for the real solutions, the cooperative solution that achieves harmony that can be sustained for as long one desires.

A Needs Filling
SKILL

JUSTIFYING

As we master juggling, we begin to involve our intelligence and justify what we want, versus what we need, in order to reasonably maintain balance in our lives. Our minds begin to lead us to validate our physically driven needs at the expense of what we innately know we really need. Only after we experience inevitable disappointments are we prepared to ultimately master the *FaithSkill* Talent of Cooperation.

A Needs Filling
ABILITY

JUGGLER

As we strive to satisfy our innately driven need for harmony through a physically based operating system, we learn to juggle the issues in our lives. We reason that as long as we have only one item on our plates, we are less likely to be out of balance. We can then develop the Skill of Justifying.

Physically Based

Intellectually Based

Spiritually Based

The Doorway connects actions to real needs

B A L A N C E

The Essential Foundation

Our Real Need

H A R M O N Y

The Fundamental Need

NOTE: Once you choose the physical, intellectual, or spiritual Personal Operating System you desire to live by, you must then master and maintain the ability, skill or talent of that System. Only then will you have the capacity to progress to the next needs filling ability, skill or talent within the system you've chosen to live by.

COOPERATION

Cooperation suggests the involvement of our entire being – body, intelligence and spirit. No one can fully cooperate without applying his or her spirit to the action.

Unfortunately, all too many do not understand this, thus, they often cooperate in only one dimension – the physical – then try to rationalize why success wasn't achieved. They do not fully commit themselves to using the talent of cooperation to satisfy the need for harmony.

As we consider the various circumstances of our lives, it is easy to see that this process requires constant effort. However, as we gain acceptance and begin to understand our purpose, we are driven to seek for stability, or harmony, by encouraging and offering cooperation whenever possible.

Our spirit knows that there must be balance if harmony is to exist; harmony must exist in order for permanence to occur.

However, we also innately know that balance can only occur when opposition is present.

As we perfect the *FaithSkill* of Cooperation, we develop an instinct for opposition, anticipating it's eminent appearance with solutions in hand for it's immediate resolve.

The *FaithSkill* of Fearlessness

The Progression from Abilities to Talents:

Once you understand the Essential Foundation of *Opposition,* you are able to master the physical *Ability* to be a Fighter, then the intellectual *Skill* of Protection, and then, ultimately, the *FaithSkill Talent* of *Fearlessness*.

can become

can become

can become

A Needs Filling
ABILITY

FIGHTER

Whenever we live a physically based life, we satisfy our need for harmony by fighting against any and all opposition that occurs in our lives. This satisfies our physical want for balance because we fought the opposition, but we soon discover that the opposition never goes away so we then develop the Skill of Protection.

Physically Based

A Needs Filling
SKILL

PROTECTION

As we think our way through our battles, we begin to realize that we must choose them more carefully in order to conserve our precious energy to protect what we've gained in this life. However, that protection isn't enough so we soon become driven from within for a more stable harmony and thus strive to master the *FaithSkill* Talent of Fearlessness.

Intellectually Based

A Needs Filling
FaithSkill
TALENT

FEARLESSNESS

When we are spirit based, we realize that we must not only acknowledge opposition, but we must respect it and deal with it fearlessly. Faith cannot be maintained when fear is present, thus, a sage individual becomes fearless in his or her approach to difficulties, knowing that these will increase his or her capacities for growth.

Spiritually Based

The Doorway
connects actions to real needs

OPPOSITION

The Essential Foundation

Our Real Need

HARMONY

The Fundamental Need

NOTE: Once you choose the physical, intellectual, or spiritual Personal Operating System you desire to live by, you must then master and maintain the ability, skill or talent of that System. Only then will you have the capacity to progress to the next needs filling ability, skill or talent within the system you've chosen to live by.

FEARLESSNESS

Fearlessness is the FaithSkill that ultimately completes our inward needs satisfying process.

Sage individuals know that harmony is impossible to achieve without the presence of opposition – it is unavoidable, but once understood, is welcomed as a refiner that purifies and improves us!

Opposition is unavoidable. Those who live a spirit based life understand this and anticipate, even welcome it. They recognize that the unique forms of opposition present in their own lives provide growth opportunities that may not come in any other way. This attitude actually encourages and sets the stage for the development of the talent of fearlessness.

The more a person studies the Essential Foundation of opposition, the sooner he or she realizes the need to face it with fearlessness.

Permanent Harmony can only be attained and maintained with the practical skill of faith that is perfectly manifested in the talent of fearlessness.

Absolutely no other method of operation can consistently harness the force of opposition for good and thus move your efforts towards your life of permanent success.

PROGRESSION OF ABILITIES TO SKILLS TO TALENTS

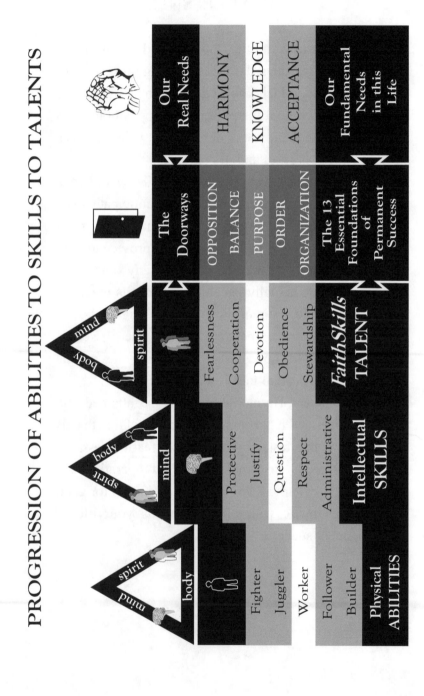

OUR PROGRESS TO DATE

Let's summarize the information we've discussed to date. As shown in the accompanying chart, we have systematically built the Leveling portion of the Essential Foundations upon the *fundamental* portion.

As you can see, by developing the talents of Fearlessness and Cooperation and adding them to Devotion, Obedience and Stewardship, you are empowered to effectively satisfy your inward *fundamental needs* for Harmony, Knowledge and Acceptance.

A step-by-step understanding and mastery of the Essential Foundations, starting with Organization, governs the evolution of these abilities to talents. It also governs our progression from a physically based life to a spiritually based life.

You see, once Organization is *understood,* one is able to *appreciate* Order. When Order is understood, Purpose can be *determined.* Once Purpose is understood, Balance is *desired.* Once Balance is desired, Opposition can be *understood* and thus effectively harnessed.

The *FaithSkill* of Reflection

The Progression from Abilities to Talents:

Once you understand the Essential Foundation of *Intelligence,* you are able to master the physical *Ability* to be a Tester, then the intellectual *Skill* of Analyzing, and then, ultimately, the *FaithSkill Talent* of *Reflection*.

can become

can become

A Needs Filling ABILITY

TESTER

In a physically based life, one finds and develops his or her intelligence by testing the environment in which he or she lives. It's an easy, effective process, however, it's very limited in its capacity to reveal the complete expanse of intelligence that we possess. So we then develop the Skill of Analyzing.

Physically Based

A Needs Filling SKILL

ANALYZING

We become analytical once we begin to develop an intellectually based life. We start to flex our brain to develop our own mind and eminently discover that intelligence is more than mere thoughts. It includes intuitions that, once understood, assist us to develop the *FaithSkill* Talent of Reflection.

Intellectually Based

A Needs Filling *FaithSkill* TALENT

REFLECTION

When we recognize our own unlimited intelligence, we begin to use the powerful talent of reflection to affirm our own immense capacity to reason. As we do, we become empowered to convert our intelligence into valuable knowledge.

Spiritually Based

The Doorway connects actions to real needs

I N T E L L I G E N C E

The Essential Foundation

Our Real Need

I D E N T I T Y

The Fundamental Need

NOTE: Once you choose the physical, intellectual, or spiritual Personal Operating System you desire to live by, you must then master and maintain the ability, skill or talent of that System. Only then will you have the capacity to progress to the next needs filling ability, skill or talent within the system you've chosen to live by.

REFLECTION

Reflection is known as the *awakening FaithSkill*.

Its refreshing attributes reinforce our spirit's will to progress by enlightening our minds to the enormous successes we regularly take for granted, as well as opening our awareness to the potential we have for future successes.

Sage individuals often utilize the powerful talent of Reflection to *spiritually* learn from experience in order to become wise. They are able to put themselves into someone else's situation and learn from it without actually being there. Such experiences can touch us to the core, which we also refer to as the *spirit*. We know that when our spirit is *touched,* our lives change. That is why reflection is such an effective teacher.

Mentors also encourage the process of proactive reflection by inviting developing Sages to ask questions and discuss information that will give further opportunities for the spirit to be touched.

Proactive reflection is the driving force in developing *FaithSkills* talents.

The more adept you become in the *FaithSkill* of reflection the greater and more rapid will be your progression towards a life of *permanent success*.

The *FaithSkill* of Humility

The Progression from Abilities to Talents:

Once you understand the Essential Foundation of *Spirit,* you are able to master the physical *Ability* to be a Wisher, then the intellectual *Skill* of Optimism, and then, ultimately, the *FaithSkill Talent* of *Humility*.

can become

can become

can become

A Needs Filling *FaithSkill* TALENT

The **Doorway** connects actions to real needs

Our Real Need

HUMILITY

A Needs Filling SKILL

OPTIMISM

When individuals fully understand the power of hope, they become humble because they discover that this originates from the spirit within them.

Hope propels them to move ahead no matter what the issues may be.

Their spirits are spirits of hope – so is yours.

S

P

I

R

I

T

I

D

E

N

T

I

T

Y

A Needs Filling ABILITY

WISHER

When physically based, individuals tend to deny their spirits' influence in their lives as it seems weak and mysterious. However, they know they feel better with hope, so they begin to manifest it by wishing. They quickly realize that hope is strong, but more is needed, so they develop the Skill of Optimism.

Smart individuals quickly discover that thinking positively will move them forward towards success. However, they all too often become content with this new ability and go no further. Only the wise realize that optimism verifies that they have much more potential than they think, so they begin to develop the *FaithSkill* Talent of Humility.

Intellectually Based

Spiritually Based

The Essential Foundation

The Fundamental Need

Physically Based

NOTE: Once you choose the physical, intellectual, or spiritual Personal Operating System you desire to live by, you must then master and maintain the ability, skill or talent of that System. Only then will you have the capacity to progress to the next needs filling ability, skill or talent within the system you've chosen to live by.

HUMILITY

Humility is the *pivotal FaithSkill* of the *FaithSkills* Personal Operating System. It is the central talent of the *stabilizing* and *identifying* portions of the entire *FaithSkills* world. Without it, progress is impossible.

Only when we surrender our physical wants to our spiritual needs, are we able to fully implement a spirit-based life and thus fully satisfy our *fundamental needs*.

These *fundamental needs* are spirit driven and must be satisfied through the same medium. Humility is the very essence of that process.

As the fuel for Hope, Humility drives us to look within and truly see what we're made of. As we do, we can be directed to reflect and awaken ourselves to our true identities – spiritual beings!

Once recognized for who we really are, we can be empowered to *act upon* our lives rather than have them act upon us through uncaring and vicious circumstances.

Through Humility, one is never the victim of circumstance, but rather a student who learns from it.

Your life becomes a constant cycle of growth from one situation to another that your spirit appreciates for the enlightenment and direction they offer.

The *FaithSkill* of Discipline

The Progression from Abilities to Talents:

Once you understand the Essential Foundation of *Body,* you are able to master the physical *Ability* to be a Player, then the intellectual *Skill* of Collaboration, and then, ultimately, the *FaithSkill Talent* of *Discipline.*

can become

can become

can become

A Needs Filling
ABILITY

PLAYER

In a physically based system, one knows that the only way to get the most out of this life is to be a participant. We do this by becoming players, so we can more clearly identify ourselves by the actions that temporarily satisfy us. It is then that we begin to develop the Skill of Collaboration.

Physically Based

A Needs Filling
SKILL

COLLABORATION

Participating isn't enough when we begin to live an intellectually based life. We need to have more involvement in the governing factors of our lives, so we become collaborators in order to identify some sort of justification for our physical existence and participation. But, we still remain unsatisfied until we begin to develop the *FaithSkill* Talent of Discipline.

Intellectually Based

A Needs Filling
FaithSkill
TALENT

DISCIPLINE

When we become humble, we realize that we must do more than participate and collaborate to understand the purpose for our bodies. We soon see the need for discipline. As we start to exercise discipline upon ourselves with our spirits, we are able to manifest our spirits' immense abilities and capacities.

Spiritually Based

The **Doorway** connects actions to real needs

B O D Y

The Essential Foundation

Our Real Need

I D E N T I T Y

The Fundamental Need

NOTE: Once you choose the physical, intellectual, or spiritual Personal Operating System you desire to live by, you must then master and maintain the ability, skill or talent of that System. Only then will you have the capacity to progress to the next needs filling ability, skill or talent within the system you've chosen to live by.

DISCIPLINE

Discipline is the *empowering FaithSkill* of the *Identifying* portion of Our *fundamental needs*.

When you truly know who you are, you strive to become a disciplined individual. By understanding the purpose of your body, which is to manifest and expand upon the nature of your spirit, you immediately develop an awareness that discipline is the only physical manifestation that demonstrates your knowledge of yourself.

Think about it. What do you tell yourself, or what does your spirit tell your mind, when you witness a supreme act of discipline? You say, *that person's got it together* – Right?

We innately know that discipline is a supreme talent that we all should strive to develop. Our spirits know that it's required in order for progression to occur, regardless of the situation.

Discipline is the only way that you will be able to actually recognize and appreciate your marvelous body.

It manifests your progression in the development of your own *FaithSkills* Personal Operating System. The more disciplined you become the more evident is the influence of your spirit in your life.

You quickly verify to yourself and others that the benefits by far outweigh the sacrifices.

PROGRESSION OF ABILITIES TO SKILLS TO TALENTS

Our Real Needs	The Doorways	FaithSkills TALENT	Intellectual SKILLS	Physical ABILITIES
IDENTITY	BODY SPIRIT INTELLIGENCE	Discipline Humility Reflection	Collaborative Optimistic Analytical	Player Wisher Tester
HARMONY	OPPOSITION BALANCE	Fearlessness Cooperation	Protective Justify	Fighter Juggler
KNOWLEDGE	PURPOSE ORDER	Devotion Obedience	Question Respect	Worker
ACCEPTANCE	ORGANIZATION	Stewardship	Administrative	Follower Builder
Our Fundamental Needs in this Life	The 13 Essential Foundations of Permanent Success			

mind body spirit

OUR PROGRESS TO DATE

Our chart now shows that we've applied the sage understanding of order and completed the *Stabilizing* portion of our *fundamental needs*.

By fully understanding The Essential Foundations of Intelligence, Spirit and Body you are able to appreciate the marvelous creation that you are and fulfill your deep need to discover your Identity.

Through the *FaithSkills* talents of Reflection, Humility and Discipline you empower yourself to manifest your spiritual nature in this physical world. As you do, you not only affirm your spirit's nature, but expand upon it by experiencing elements your spirit was previously unable to understand before it gained this physical body.

Your self-esteem is not only formed through these understandings and talents – it is greatly enhanced. You feel at peace with yourself and who you are. You're also able to begin seeing yourself as the person you know you *really* are.

That is why these *stabilizing* foundations are known as the patterns of confidence. You now not only *know* that all this knowledge of *permanent success* is good, but *how* and *why* it is good. You're now empowered to apply it fully in your life. As you master them, so increases your confidence.

Your spirit blossoms. Your actions become more certain and your decisions more distinct. Everyone who comes in contact with you benefits due to the comfort you provide with your inspiring actions that are firm and always fair.

The *FaithSkill* of Honesty

The Progression from Abilities to Talents:

Once you understand the Essential Foundation of *Laws,* you are able to master the physical *Ability* to be a Complier, then the intellectual *Skill* of Attentiveness, and then, ultimately, the *FaithSkill Talent* of *Honesty*.

can become

can become

A Needs Filling
ABILITY

COMPLIER

We all quickly learn that laws govern this world. When physically based in our operating style, we tend to comply with the laws only to avoid unwanted consequences, which they will surely deliver. However, when we start to recognize that laws can be a benefit, we develop the Skill of Attentiveness.

Physically Based

A Needs Filling
SKILL

ATTENTIVENESS

When we evolve to an intellectually based operating system, we become very attentive to laws in order to manipulate them and get what we want. With our mind, we analyze and study the technicalities of the laws in order to get the most out of this life. But the results are shallow so our innate need for direction is left wanting. Thus we are lead to develop the *FaithSkill* Talent of Honesty.

Intellectually Based

A Needs Filling
FaithSkill
TALENT

HONESTY

When we are spiritually based, we realize that laws are roadmaps to success, not determiners of success.
Honesty allows us to understand the laws upon which our desired successes are built.
We are capable of orchestrating successes. When honesty rules, laws guide our spirits to make success – permanently!

Spiritually Based

The Doorway connects actions to real needs

L
A
W
S

The Essential Foundation

Our Real Need

D
I
R
E
C
T
I
O
N

The Fundamental Need

NOTE: Once you choose the physical, intellectual, or spiritual Personal Operating System you desire to live by, you must then master and maintain the ability, skill or talent of that System. Only then will you have the capacity to progress to the next needs filling ability, skill or talent within the system you've chosen to live by.

HONESTY

Honesty is the dominant *FaithSkill* for satisfying the *outward* portion of our *fundamental needs*.

It is the first of the *empowering* category of *FaithSkills* talents – one that also originates from our spirits. It profoundly influences the spirits of others who come in contact with us or surround us on a regular basis.

In order to master this talent, an individual must fully understand the Essential Foundation of *Laws* so that he or she may be empowered by it rather than being governed by it.

Once we know how to conduct ourselves from within by applying the inward Foundations (organization, order, purpose, balance, opposition) to our now clearly identified being, we are capable of applying ourselves to this physical dimension in which we live. We do so through laws because our spirits know that a law predicates every success; Honesty empowers these Laws.

The *FaithSkill* of Valiance

The Progression from Abilities to Talents:

Once you understand the Essential Foundation of *Agency,* you are able to master the physical *Ability* to be a Chooser, then the intellectual *Skill* of Decisiveness, and then, ultimately, the *FaithSkill Talent* of *Valiance*.

can become *can become*

A Needs Filling
ABILITY

CHOOSER

In a physical Personal Operating System, people tend to satisfy their need for empowerment by making choices. It is this basic expression of agency that awakens us to desire more empowerment over our lives. We can then progress to develop the Skill of Decisiveness.

Physically Based

A Needs Filling
SKILL

DECISIVENESS

We grow in our ability to make decisive choices by implementing all of the previously mastered skills. By flexing our growing intellect, we perceive ourselves as having the capacity to make firm and solid decisions, but our hearts are not in the decisions we make. So we realize the need to develop the *FaithSkill* Talent of Valiance.

Intellectually Based

A Needs Filling
FaithSkill
TALENT

VALIANCE

When we're spirit based, we not only make decisions but we make them valiantly. Our capacity to exercise true agency by choosing between right and wrong is enhanced by this valiant nature. Our whole being chooses and thus determines the circumstances of our lives.

Spiritually Based

The Doorway connects actions to real needs

A G E N C Y

The Essential Foundation

Our Real Need

E M P O W E R M E N T

The Fundamental Need

NOTE: Once you choose the physical, intellectual, or spiritual Personal Operating System you desire to live by, you must then master and maintain the ability, skill or talent of that System. Only then will you have the capacity to progress to the next needs filling ability, skill or talent within the system you've chosen to live by.

VALIANCE

Valiance is the manifestation of the spirit's will through the actions of our lives. There is nothing more powerful than a valiant execution of actions to stir the hearts of people to rise to a cause and overcome opposition. Our spirits recognize this spiritually based trait and respond to the familiarity it creates by seeking to follow and duplicate it.

Regardless of differences or boundaries, valiance will penetrate them and produce affection and respect, especially when agency is used for its ultimate purpose – to choose right over wrong, or good over evil. This process satisfies our *fundamental need* for empowerment.

Valiance is the physical manifestation of the spiritual power of passion. Action fueled by this FaithSkill is powerful and fulfilling to the souls of many individuals who live in this wonderful world.

Once our spirit knows the directions or laws that govern this life, it wants to be empowered by valiantly exercising its will through authentic actions.

The *FaithSkill* of Authenticity

The Progression from Abilities to Talents:

Once you understand the Essential Foundation of **Action**, you are able to master the physical **Ability** to be a Doer, then the intellectual **Skill** of Diligence, and then, ultimately, the **FaithSkill** **Talent** of **Authenticity**.

can become

can become

A Needs Filling **ABILITY**

DOER

When living in a physically based operating system, the way to satisfy your innate need for empowerment is to be a doer. You do many different things, hoping to feel empowered by your accomplishments, but soon you realize you need more, so you develop the Skill of Diligence.

Physically Based

A Needs Filling **SKILL**

DILIGENCE

Once we realize that agency empowers us, we take diligent actions. This diligence increases the quality and quantity of satisfaction we gain from our actions. However, we soon learn that only genuine actions count; thus we strive to develop the *FaithSkill* Talent of Authenticity.

Intellectually Based

A Needs Filling *FaithSkill* **TALENT**

AUTHENTICITY

Actions that are authentic are the ones that touch the spirits of others. We satisfy our need for empowerment fully when we can exercise our spirits' wills in ways that will form permanence, as authentic actions do. This is when actions really do speak clearly.

Spiritually Based

The Doorway connects actions to real needs

A C T I O N

The Essential Foundation

Our **Real** **Need**

E M P O W E R M E N T

The Fundamental Need

NOTE: Once you choose the physical, intellectual, or spiritual Personal Operating System you desire to live by, you must then master and maintain the ability, skill or talent of that System. Only then will you have the capacity to progress to the next needs filling ability, skill or talent within the system you've chosen to live by.

AUTHENTICITY

Authenticity is the *FaithSkill* that solidifies our actions and creates permanent influences upon those that we are empowered to guide, lead or nurture.

No matter who we are, there is someone who counts on our actions to fill their own *fundamental needs*. When those actions are authentic, they satisfy those needs permanently.

Authenticity is an attribute that only the spirit can recognize. When it does, it is moved to reciprocate, which is why genuine people attract genuine people.

This talent empowers the humble, disciplined, honest and valiant of this world to establish bonds here that will last for eternity.

Authenticity converts simple actions into powerful communicators that stir the souls of men to rise above their failings and strive to duplicate what they've experienced.

Nothing – absolutely nothing – will satisfy the spirit's need for empowerment more than authentic actions.

PROGRESSION OF ABILITIES TO SKILLS TO TALENTS

Physical ABILITIES	Intellectual SKILLS	*FaithSkills* TALENT	The Doorways	Our Real Needs
Doer	Diligent	Authenticity	ACTION	EMPOWERMENT
Chooser	Decisive	Valiance	AGENCY	
Complier	Attentive	Honesty	LAWS	DIRECTION
Player	Collaborative	Discipline	BODY	IDENTITY
Wisher	Optimistic	Humility	SPIRIT	
Tester	Analytical	Reflection	INTELLIGENCE	
Fighter	Protective	Fearlessness	OPPOSITION	HARMONY
Juggler	Justify	Cooperation	BALANCE	
Worker	Question	Devotion	PURPOSE	KNOWLEDGE
Follower	Respect	Obedience	ORDER	ACCEPTANCE
Builder	Administrative	Stewardship	ORGANIZATION	
			The 13 Essential Foundations of Permanent Success	Our Fundamental Needs in this Life

mind · spirit · body

body · spirit · mind

mind · body · spirit

OUR PROGRESS TO DATE

The progressive chart displays that the critical *empowering* foundations of Laws, Agency and Action, which satisfy the *fundamental needs* for Direction and Empowerment, are now completed and solidly built upon the *identifying* foundations.

It is important for you to remember that satisfying *fundamental needs* through the Essential Foundations is only possible when previous needs have already been met through previous foundations, and likewise when skills are built upon the foundation of previous skills.

Think about it! Can Valiance or Authenticity occur in a dishonest environment? Or can devotion be sustained without obedience? Likewise, can Agency empower Action for a sustained period without a solid understanding and commitment to Purpose? No! Neither can Purpose be maintained without a solid desire to implement Organization through Order. It is absolutely impossible! It is a progressive process that must occur in a specific order if success is to be achieved.

Once we are at peace with who we are, we can empower our spirits to be involved in our daily actions. Then, our Fundamental *empowering* needs can be effectively and permanently satisfied by the enduring *FaithSkills* of Honesty, Valiance and Authenticity.

Now, let us complete the system by adding the *resulting* and *governing* categories of the *FaithSkills* talents, namely, Cultivation and Faithfulness. They satisfy our most powerful need for Fulfillment or Achievement.

The *FaithSkill* of Cultivation

The Progression from Abilities to Talents:

Once you understand the Essential Foundation of **The Harvest,** you are able to master the physical **Ability** to be a Taker, then the intellectual **Skill** of productivity, and then, ultimately, the **FaithSkill Talent** of **Cultivation**.

can become

can become

A Needs Filling
ABILITY

TAKER

As a physically based individual, one looks out for him or herself and takes whatever is perceived to make him or her feel satisfied. In time, such individuals realize the short-sightedness of this approach, so they become prepared to develop the Skill of Productivity.

Physically Based

A Needs Filling
SKILL

PRODUCTIVITY

Once we progress to an intellectually based method of operation, we use our minds to justify taking a larger portion of the harvest because of the productivity that we feel we have contributed. But that too provides short-term satisfaction, so we develop the *FaithSkill* Talent of Cultivation.

Intellectually Based

A Needs Filling
FaithSkill
TALENT

CULTIVATION

As we become spirit based, we unselfishly recognize the enormous value of concentrating on preparing for the harvest rather than focusing on the harvest itself. We begin to orchestrate successes. Because we design them, we feel a deep sense of achievement from the confidence that these results eminently provide.

Spiritually Based

The Doorway connects actions to real needs

T H E

H A R V E S T

The Essential Foundation

Our Real Need

F U L F I L L M E N T

The Fundamental Need

NOTE: Once you choose the physical, intellectual, or spiritual Personal Operating System you desire to live by, you must then master and maintain the ability, skill or talent of that System. Only then will you have the capacity to progress to the next needs filling ability, skill or talent within the system you've chosen to live by.

CULTIVATION

Cultivation is the *FaithSkill* talent that openly manifests your spirit's goodwill. It makes implementation of The resulting Essential Foundation of *the harvest* not only possible, but also bountiful.

The powerful *caring, nurturing* and *giving* influence of cultivation inspires those who witness it and transforms those who exercise it into individuals who are not only productive but inspiring. Their very presence can *move* people to want to improve themselves and their levels of performance.

This *FaithSkill* guarantees results that are satisfying to the spirit's immense need for Fulfillment, or Achievement, because of the eminent and always bountiful results of the *permanent success* it creates. This *FaithSkill* assures self-reliance and fuels self-esteem to levels that are unattainable through any other abilities or skills.

Development of this *FaithSkills* talent provides the *cement* of *permanent success* because it provides so much for others. It's very essence – giving – is the benefit of absolutely everyone who comes in contact with you.

Your influence is unavoidable!

The *FaithSkill* of Faithfulness

The Progression from Abilities to Talents:

Once you understand the Essential Foundation of *Commitment,* you are able to master the physical *Ability* to be Present, then the intellectual *Skill* of Trustworthiness, and then, ultimately, the *FaithSkill Talent* of *Faithfulness*.

can become

can become

A Needs Filling
FaithSkill
TALENT

The **Doorway** connects actions to real needs

Our **Real Need**

A Needs Filling
SKILL

FAITHFULNESS

TRUSTWORTHINESS

A Needs Filling
ABILITY

PRESENT

We evolve from simply being present to becoming someone that can be counted on, even trusted, to contribute to the harvest. However, when the actual harvest may be in question, our intellectually based method of operation will justify its failure and reason alternatives. But our spirit knows that that isn't right, so we grow to ultimately develop the *FaithSkill* Talent of Faithfulness.

The spirit knows that commitment not only ensures a harvest but deserves one. The only way to fully commit the spirit is through the talent of faithfulness. "Where there's a will, there's a way" comes to life when we exercise the *FaithSkill* Talent of Faithfulness. It literally empowers the spirit to act in our daily lives.

From a physically based point of view, one quickly figures out that being present is the sure way to get a portion of the harvest. However, we soon find out that being present doesn't assure a consistent harvest from which to take, thus we progress in our understanding to develop the Skill of Trustworthiness.

C O M M I T M E N T

F U L F I L L M E N T

Physically Based

Intellectually Based

Spiritually Based

The Essential Foundation

The Fundamental Need

NOTE: Once you choose the physical, intellectual, or spiritual Personal Operating System you desire to live by, you must then master and maintain the ability, skill or talent of that System. Only then will you have the capacity to progress to the next needs filling ability, skill or talent within the system you've chosen to live by.

FAITHFULNESS

No other *FaithSkill* impacts us more than the talent of Faithfulness. It is the result of applying into our lives all of the previous *FaithSkills* talents – it is the culminating one that *governs* our level of fulfillment.

Its all-encompassing nature completes the Foundation of commitment like no other FaithSkill does for any other Foundation. Through diligent implementation, Faithfulness ensures completion, or success. Our lives become full when we know that others are faithful to us, because we know this occurs only when the spirits of others unconditionally accept our spirit for what it is. It's a form of true love that our spirit yearns for.

When we are faithful to others, we gain a deep sense of completion and purpose knowing that we are contributing at a level that far exceeds the abilities of our bodies and minds.

Commitment takes on much more meaning when we evolve from just being present, to being trustworthy, to being Faithful.

Many of us think that trustworthiness completes the fulfillment of the foundation of commitment. It doesn't, however, unless the spirit is involved. That is why when we progress to an intellectually based life, we reason that we need to document commitments or retain physical possessions in order to assure commitment, when in fact such actions frustrate it and cause us to become disillusioned – to avoid trusting anyone or anything.

We also reason in our minds that justice will restore order. Instead, we find that it too is formed upon physical parameters, and thus cannot satisfy our spirit's need for fulfillment.

It is only when we operate at the spiritual level that we appreciate how Faithfulness applies in completing the *governing* category of The Essential Foundations.

Powerful as it is, the awesome influence of Faithfulness can only be implemented and sustained once it has been *cultivated* by *authentic actions* that can be *valiantly* expressed, if required, by *honest, disciplined, humbled* individuals. They have *reflected* and decided that they will *fearlessly cooperate* and *devote* themselves to being *obedient* to you, if necessary, as they support you in the s*tewardship* of your life to help you create successes that can endure throughout all of time, or in other words, Permanently. And that requires you to exercise faith in yourself!

We've made amazing progress! Your achievement is incredible. You should be well pleased with yourself!

What you've revealed to yourself, to your mind and soul, is familiar to your spirit. It knows that there is a pattern, a way, that is simple to understand and *doable* for you – for anyone who sincerely strives to create a state of being known as *permanent success*.

It's real. It's possible!

Now, let's look at the complete *enchilada* with the chart on the next page.

PROGRESSION OF ABILITIES TO SKILLS TO TALENTS

BODY	MIND	SPIRIT	The Doorways	Our Real Needs
Present	Trustworthy	Faithfulness	COMMITMENT	FULFILLMENT
Taker	Productive	Cultivation	THE HARVEST	
Doer	Diligent	Authenticity	ACTION	EMPOWERMENT
Chooser	Decisive	Valiance	AGENCY	
Complier	Attentive	Honesty	LAWS	DIRECTION
Player	Collaborative	Discipline	BODY	IDENTITY
Wisher	Optimistic	Humility	SPIRIT	
Tester	Analytical	Reflection	INTELLIGENCE	
Fighter	Protective	Fearlessness	OPPOSITION	HARMONY
Juggler	Justify	Cooperation	BALANCE	
Worker	Question	Devotion	PURPOSE	KNOWLEDGE
Follower	Respect	Obedience	ORDER	ACCEPTANCE
Builder	Administrative	Stewardship	ORGANIZATION	
Physical ABILITIES	Intellectual SKILLS	*FaithSkills* TALENT	The 13 Essential Foundations of Permanent Success	Our Fundamental Needs in this Life

259

Rene Says

Faith can always remove fear from your life. When you exercise faith, fear cannot exist. Faith and fear are generated from intangible planes but act upon your tangible life. Fear comes from your mind and acts upon your spirit through your body. When you allow fear to exist within yourself you're allowing life to act upon you. On the other hand, when you choose to exercise faith, you're empowering yourself to act upon your life. When exercising faith, you choose to have your spirit act upon your body, often without the involvement of your intelligence. This is the reason why faith is often hard for the mind to grasp. We've all unconsciously done this at some point in

Continued next page...

Note how it lists all of the needs, foundations, abilities, skills and talents and shows their interrelationship.

Notice that the three systems are listed as Personal Operating Systems. Does this mean that the system you choose to develop, as a result of adapting and adopting this information, could be different than the one I use? Absolutely! Why? Because we're all at different levels of knowledge, understanding and experience.

Do you remember that we stated earlier that good teachers recognize that students have different levels of knowledge and understanding, thus, they begin to teach from *where the students are*?

We've tried to begin this summary of *FaithSkills* from *where you are* – to present the information in the *bite-sized* pieces that can help you relate to it in your own way. It has to be meaningful to you, personally, otherwise this program becomes like many others – externally imposed, instead of internally sanctioned and applied.

Notice that the *FaithSkills* are represented by words that are already familiar to you.

Note also that a picture has been presented in the form of a chart, because we know that a *picture is worth a*

260

thousand words!

As you *liken* the *FaithSkills* Personal Operating System unto yourself through this chart, you may finally be able to understand why your efforts don't seem to be self sustaining, and why harmony seems to be so elusive when you try protecting your successes.

Hopefully, you are now able to understand why you're on the *treadmill* of success, rather than *being* the *permanent success* that you desire and can become.

It's a process – one that can sometimes seem confusing to complete. However, we have provided direction through the *compass* of *permanent success* – *FaithSkills* – and the *True North* of *permanent success* – The Essential Foundations.

They guide you and nurture you to systematically and personally build your own *FaithSkills* Personal Operating System – one that can empower you to apply your entire self to this life and enable you to form the virtues of True Leadership.

Rene Says

our lives when we say to ourselves, "I don't know why I did that, but I *just knew* that I had to." Our wills are so strong that they actually take over our physical beings and propel them to do what our wills know has to be done. Great acts of courage often take place under such circumstances and touch the lives of many. So, the next time you recognize that fear is entering your life, exercise faith by not only consciously allowing your spirit to govern your actions, but knowingly orchestrating the process so it can influence the thoughts that occupy the rooms of your mind. You'll be amazed at how fear will diminish to a manageable and healthy stimulant of caution by which your actions can be governed.

Pro-Active Reflection

CHAPTER

20

True Leadership

"Lead By The Heart and Manage The Mind"

*N*o other phrase more clearly defines what True Leadership is and what it does. It's an expression that deeply moved me when I first heard it. I was intrigued with its effects upon my heart and mind as I circulated its comforting tones between my intelligence and spirit.

I pondered – what is True Leadership? To me it was an oxymoronic term, like jumbo shrimp, or a whimsical envy like Shangri-La. But my spirit pounded through my heart an affirmation that it was indeed possible. Yet, how could two words evoke such a unique combination of emotions and reflective thoughts all at the same time?

My mind tried to justify this seemingly illogical thought – truth in leadership didn't exist anymore; I just had to look at all too many local and global leaders to validate this; yet, I *knew* in my mind that it existed.

So I decided to examine the two words individually – here's what I discovered.

True is defined with such words as: "real, genuine, authentic, essential, faithful, reliable, fundamental, loyal and truthful".

Sound like *FaithSkills*?

Leadership is often defined with words such as: "guidance, direction, inspire, to be ahead, to be first and one".

More *FaithSkills*?

True Leadership then, is the result of the *FaithSkills* talents and the virtues they develop. Let's take a closer look at how this on-going process of developing true leadership through virtues works.

Think back to chapter 5, entitled *Down to the Basics*. There we explained that you could effectively satisfy your *fundamental need* for *Acceptance* by utilizing the Essential Foundations of Organization and Order. They, in turn, develop the FaithSkills of Stewardship and Obedience, which then convert your physical needs-filling actions into deep spiritual power known as the virtue of Discernment, the first of the seven virtues.

When you discern, you are able to *see distinctly, distinguish mentally, see the difference between (two or more things)*. This virtue becomes refined as you learn to become sage. Sages carefully consider what needs to be organized for the common good, then they apply themselves through the Essential Foundations that will achieve their purposes.

Does this method of leadership sound like it might positively influence others? I'm sure you will agree that it does. If you were part of a team where the leader was a discerning individual, as described above, would you want to follow that leader? Likely so, because you know that he or she considers the interests and needs of the whole team when moving it forward (because of the FaithSkill of stewardship), and not just his or her own. They know that the *greater good includes their good.*

Remember that this is only one of the characteristics of a virtue. Virtues touch and influence others because they are formed from our three dimensional being – intelligence, spirit and body. They are characteristics that are often referred to as spirits because they are physically formed with sincere considerations that touch the spirits of others and thus literally *move* them. People who are touched by virtues not only desire to improve themselves, they actually do improve themselves because of the profound exampling nature of virtues.

Have a look at the following illustration. It explains how our being acts as a prism for *FaithSkills* as they are applied through us with the Essential Foundations.

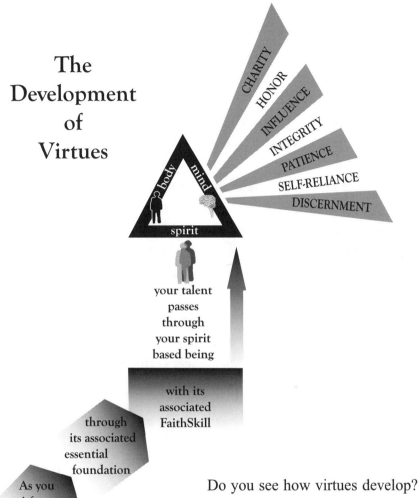

The
Development
of
Virtues

CHARITY
HONOR
INFLUENCE
INTEGRITY
PATIENCE
SELF-RELIANCE
DISCERNMENT

body · mind · spirit

your talent
passes
through
your spirit
based being

with its
associated
FaithSkill

through
its associated
essential
foundation

As you
satisfy your
fundamental
need

Do you see how virtues develop? A simple process, right? However, simple doesn't mean easy. Just like what happens to pure light when it passes through a prism of pure crystal. The purer the crystal (us), the more distinct the results of the refraction that takes place. It also applies to the light that is applied (our actions) through the prism. The purer the light, the more vivid the spectrum. *FaithSkills* are pure. So are the Essential Foundations. You are the only remaining variable. Will you live a spirit based life and provide a pure prism for the benefit of others?

Remember that discernment is only the first of seven virtues, each of which has its own power to influence and change lives. They are gradually built, one upon another in consecutive order, until they culminate in the 7th virtue of charity.

You've likely already recognized some of the huge benefits that come from developing these virtues. Here are several more.

Look at the words often used to define virtues: Effective Force, Power, Righteousness, Beneficial Quality, Moral Excellence, Example and Excellence.

Pretty awesome attributes, wouldn't you agree? If you demonstrated these attributes, would other people see you in a different light? Would you see yourself in a different light? Absolutely! You can have them all as you consistently work on developing your *FaithSkills* based life!

Let's now have a look at a complete listing of the virtues developed through the *FaithSkills* Success Building process. As you will see, it is a process like no other before it. Have a look at the chart.

The Success Building Process of Virtues

As you satisfy the Fundamental Need of:	Through the Essential Foundation of:	By Exercising the FaithSkill of:	You Build the Virtue of:
	Commitment	Faithfulness Cultivation	CHARITY
Fulfillment	The Harvest	Authenticity	HONOR
	Action	Valiance	
Empowerment	Agency	Honesty	INFLUENCE
	Laws	Discipline	
Direction	Body	Humility	INTEGRITY
	Spirit	Reflection	
Identity	Intelligence	Fearlessness	PATIENCE
	Opposition	Cooperation	
Harmony	Balance	Devotion	SELF-RELIANCE
	Purpose	Obedience	DISCERNMENT
Knowledge	Order	Stewardship	
Acceptance	Organization		

As we've mentioned previously, there's a pattern to achieving *permanent success*. The same applies for True Leadership. What's most exciting is that True Leadership is a direct result of effectively patterning *FaithSkills*. It's the barometer, the mirror, if you will, for accessing your progress towards developing your own Personal Operating System – one justifies the other. So, as you can see, if you

– improve your *FaithSkills* you improve your true leadership style;

Rene Says

Achieving goals is much easier when you transport them through a logical progression from their spiritual to intellectual to physical existences. With your knowledge, you intellectually form your objectives. You then convert them into desires and transfer them into their spiritual realm where they begin to form in your heart in preparation for transfer to the physical realm. This is where most people drop the ball. They don't understand that this is where all of the preparation for change takes place. Change must occur if goals are to be reached. You need to form what your mind's eye sees in your heart. As you visualize your goal, you must start to *act it* into its physical being. You start doing this by writing it down on paper. This gives it

Continued next page...

– improve your true leadership style you increase the positive influence you have on others;

– increase the positive influence you have on others, you increase the acceptance of yourself as a leader/mentor. This will motivate you to improve your exercising of your own *FaithSkills* which begins the perpetuation of your *FaithSkills* Personal Operation System.

It doesn't just *happen* on its own – that's probably why so many haven't discovered it. Rest assured, it does exist, but it can only happen by strategically exercising your will.

Let me open your awareness another way on how the very essence of the *FaithSkills* Personal Operating System, *exercising faith in* yourself and others, creates these powerful virtues, and thus, True Leadership.

Reflect for a moment. Where have you *experienced* these virtues in action? You know, who *touched* you with some or all of these virtues: Discernment, Self-Reliance, Patience, Integrity, Honor, Influence and Charity? Who used these virtues to *exercise faith* in you like no one else could?

If you're like any other human life form that I know, only one person comes

270

to mind – Mom!

That's Right! Effective and committed Mothers are the ones who develop the pattern of True Leadership much more rapidly and naturally than men. They have an advantage, because if they choose to, they are able to draw on their intuitively spiritual natures in all of their actions.

No one, absolutely no one, has more potential to "lead by the heart and manage the mind" than a woman in the royal position of Mother. She can literally form the future of the nations in which we live; that's True Leadership.

Mothering is a personal operating style that effectively combines the physical, intellectual and spiritual parts of our beings in a way that can influence others for a lifetime.

Think about it. For those of you who had a committed Mom, don't the effects of her stewardship still affect you today?

This *mothering* style is powerful when done effectively because it naturally breeds loyalty through its spiritual essence and drives people to rise to excellence by its exampling, not for glory, but for deep personal commitment that manifests love.

Yes, True Leadership is love. I'm not

Rene Says

physical form. Then you begin to speak of it in terms of *when* not *if,* such as "Sir, *when* you're having me do this repair for you, do you want me to also do the following?" or "*When* I start working with you, will I be able to expand my skills in…?" You see, for me it has always been "When I publish my book I will …" It has never been "if I publish my book". Once I formed my goal clearly in my mind's eye, I spent years developing it. I call this *speaking it into the past.* Adoption of this method of success building is effective in the art of sales management and leadership. Try it! You'll be pleased with the results. Be patient, have faith in yourself. It takes time, as all preparation does, but it works. After all, you are reading this book, aren't you?

talking about romance. I'm talking about pure love, which is the unconditional acceptance of your spirit by another spirit. This basic foundational need for acceptance must be satisfied first, otherwise, the rest of our needs-filling processes will inevitably collapse. When it is satisfied, however, the doors are opened for fulfilling the rest of our *fundamental needs.*

True leaders genuinely accept those whom they lead as spiritual beings that are precious, thus they always treat them as equal beings and respect them as fellow *explorers* who are simply trying to discover and improve themselves through this journey we call life.

Those who are lead by True Leaders are driven to excel and attain incredible goals and successes that are not easily achieved by other methods.

Now I realize that some of you may not have had positive experiences with your Mother's personal Mothering style – I didn't either – so I can appreciate that it may be more difficult for you to relate to what I'm talking about. But you have likely observed good mothering and recognize the incredible influence it can have – I did. So there's no excuse for not striving to develop this incredibly beneficial style of leadership.

This brings us to two interesting points. Firstly, just because you're a woman, doesn't necessarily mean that you're going to be a great mother or leader. You have an advantage over a man due to your spiritual tendencies and nature, but it doesn't mean that you're a shoo-in. If you do not have the desire, or lack the understanding to develop your abilities, skills and talents so you can exercise faith in yourself or others, it just won't happen.

Secondly, you may not be a mother through the process of giving birth. Does that mean you are incapable of *mothering*? No! You can still have those nurturing gifts and use them in different settings.

Guys! That's why Parenting is without a doubt the most important leadership position you can ever hold.

Sincerely attempt to parent and you'll not only develop from within like you never thought possible, but you'll also gain a unique perspective of your own spiritual dimension.

Notice I didn't say *successfully* parent, as this is difficult to measure at any given point in time – you do the best you can with the knowledge you have at the time!

Parenting is an on-going process that requires more than just the physical or intellectual being – it also requires the spiritual. When all three of your dimensions are involved, and your *FaithSkills* and virtues are developing, you can offer True Leadership to your parenting efforts. The only difference between parenting and any other leadership assignment is that parenting never ends. You can never be fully removed from, or relinquish, the role of parent. Success, on the other hand, will leave you the moment you disobey its required disciplines.

Now let's make sure that you clearly understand the information I've presented so far in this chapter. *Mothering, Fathering* and *Parenting* are the styles that most closely duplicate the *FaithSkills* Operating System, because they are the results of spiritually based Personal Operating Systems that promote the skill of exercising faith in yourself and others, and thus have the potential to achieve *permanent success* from this life.

Sorry, guys, but women are *more endowed* with the capacity for True Leadership because of their natural spiritual sensitivities. These are manifested in the *Mothering* Personal Operating style.

Study after study is proving that women who are placed into positions of leadership earn higher scores in acceptance, loyalty and respect than men.

Consider the recent study from Leeds University in England. It found that "women bosses not only inspire others and solve complex problems better than men, they're also more accessible".

Laura Graves from the University of Connecticut stated, "women are better at individual consideration, they're better at working with their subordinates, assessing his or her needs, and helping them develop".

Alimo Metcalfe from Leeds also confirmed that "even men find women to be better bosses" according to their study of over 2,000 British men and women*.

Women do seem to have the edge. But, please be clear, it's not because of their gender, it's because of their method of operation, *Mothering*, which uses the same talents and Foundations filling the same *fundamental needs* as *FaithSkills*.

I know from first hand experience that this is true. After being thrown into several years of single parenting, I quickly realized that I was often lacking in the spiritual sensitivities required to successfully meet *fundamental needs* through the foundations, in order to develop much needed *FaithSkills* and virtues.

I also learned to greatly admire the courage of single moms. They have a myriad of concerns that constantly drain their spiritual reservoirs, sometimes making it difficult for them to use their *Mothering* Personal Operating Systems the way they'd like to.

Those who intend to go into business, male or female, should study the art of single parenting from a mom's perspective for a year or so before they go into business. Then they will know what it *really* takes to be a True Leader who can make a business a solid success.

In summary, *Mothering* is the best term to describe the style that you develop as you form and apply a *FaithSkills* Personal Operating System.

To be sure that you've really understood how this concept applies in real life, we'd like to share two examples with you. Here's the first scenario.

---

* Research provided by University of Leeds management professor Beverly Alimo - Metcalfe and researcher John Alban - Metcalfe, who surveyed 2,000 British men and women in middle and senior management positions.

You own a textile business that employs 20 people.

Over the years, you've cultivated their loyalty and earned their respect. It's late on Thursday afternoon and you receive a huge order that is totally unexpected. You know it will take several days of round-the-clock work to get the order out by Monday.

What are you going to do? Your first thought is to simply tell your employees that they have to work this weekend – no choice. But you can't do that – it wouldn't be fair, nor would it necessarily be the most profitable way to go considering the potential for paying out double overtime. Besides, you've built good relationships with them that you don't want to destroy.

So, the first thing you do is ask them all to meet in the lunchroom. You ask one of the men to take notes from the meeting because you know that everyone, including you, appreciates Total Honest Communication. Besides memory is not a reliable communicator. You explain the situation clearly, then invite suggestions from the team. They offer a number of possibilities. You all discuss the positives and negatives of each one, then narrow down the list to the one that everyone feels is best.

You are humbled to realize that everyone is willing to give up portions of their days off to fill this order – they decide to share the workload to avoid anyone losing a major portion of their time off. They also want to eliminate the payment of double overtime in order to preserve the substantial profit the order will provide.

As the weekend work progresses, you treat with pizza and doughnuts to cement the bonding relationship that's occurring. You foster a great camaraderie – more laughing, more patience, more disciplined effort, more devotion to achieving the common goal.

Do you reach your goal? Absolutely – the hundreds of boxes waiting for shipment are proof of that. So are your exhausted workers!

Did your *mothering* style operating system make a difference? Absolutely! Just as it has many times before.

Have you had the good fortune of experiencing this approach? Possibly you've even used it yourself, not consciously realizing what you were actually doing.

Let's consider in detail how a *Mothering* style of *FaithSkills* Personal Operating System was applied by the owner of the textile business.

First, consider *fundamental needs*. How was the need for Knowledge met? (The owner honestly presented the details of the situation and invited input from the team.) Direction? (The possibilities were discussed, the *plan of attack* outlined and the expectations noted.) Empowerment? (The team members were invited to offer their suggestions and what they were willing to do to meet the goal.)

Next, the Essential Foundations. Here are examples of two of them. See if you can find examples of the others. Organization – the owner gathered the team together so they could discuss the situation and organize a plan. Balance – the owner and the team together determined how the time and work could be divided so that everyone shared the responsibility – no one had to give their all, but everyone was invited to give something to ensure the success of the project.

How about the *FaithSkills talents* and the *virtues* they produce? For instance, did you notice the owner's Humility? (He asked his employees for answers – he didn't assume that he had them all.) His Honesty? (He had a problem that he clearly explained to his team members because he truly wanted their input. He gave honesty and got honesty back as the team members stated their willingness to avoid the payment of double overtime in order to preserve the profits that would result and definitely reflect the bonuses.) His Integrity? (He shared the profits generated by the common effort with relative bonuses as he always had before.)

His Charity? The owner knew his employees were entitled to days off – he didn't dictate that they had to work. Instead, he invited them to take some ownership for the problem so they could determine their own responses.

Our second example involves a single mother and her 16-year-old daughter. The daughter is anxious to buy a car and has asked her mother's input.

As they sit down together, the daughter leads the discussion, with the encouragement of the mother.

The daughter explains that she really wants the independence that owning a car would bring. She has a job now and feels ready to take on this responsibility. She explains that if she had a car, she wouldn't have to ask her mother for rides anymore, plus, she could also drive her younger brother to Cubs and other events so the mother would have more free time. She also reminds her mother about the great car they both looked at, at the lot near the mall. The daughter then invites her mother's comments.

The mother first explains that she understands her daughter's desire for independence – she was 16 once! She also acknowledges that her daughter is a responsible person, that she would take care of a car, and also be a great chauffeur.

She then asks her daughter what kinds of expenses she thinks would be involved. The daughter explains that these would include the cost of the car ($3,000), gas and insurance. She also reminds her mom that she's been saving her money so she could buy a car.

Her mother expresses her pride in the girl for saving her money for a future purchase. She then reminds her that the girl's grandmother is selling her car for $1,000, which would be an excellent buy. It would also be easier on gas than the car on the lot, and would cost less for insurance because of its age.

The daughter explains that grandma's car is pretty old and rather strange looking, so she'd rather not be seen in it. She'd rather drive

Rene Says

As a parent, manager, or owner/operator, have you ever wondered how you're doing in your position of leadership? I do – daily. Here's a method I use to assess my performance. I ask myself this question. "Do I sufficiently empower the people for whom I am responsible to allow them to fully utilize their agency?" In other words, do I organize the environment and myself so they can follow a pattern that encourages progress? You see, as a steward you are responsible for setting the stage correctly so you can determine whether or not your team members are

Continued next page...

the fancier, newer car they saw on the lot.

Her mother asks her about her monthly budget for the car. As she's explaining, the mom takes out her checkbook to show her daughter the last three months of expenses for the family car. The daughter is surprised to see the bills for tires, the regular oil change, and the brakes that needed repairing. Even the cost of gas is much higher than she thought it would be. She comments that she didn't think about *that kind of stuff.*

She also admits that she doesn't have quite enough to buy the car she really likes and pay for the insurance too – she was hoping to borrow money from mom.

The mother then asks her daughter how she would pay back that money and take care of car expenses too.

She suggests that her daughter summarize the information discussed so far so that all of the options are clear.

As the daughter does this, she mentions that with all those possible expenses, she couldn't have any fun because there would be nothing left from her paycheck. She asks her mother what she thinks would be the best thing to do.

The mother reminds her daughter that although she is very capable and responsible, the costs involved might suggest that buying a car should be put off until a later date. But she knows that the daughter is totally capable and should make the decision on her own. Whatever she decided, mom would support her because she had honestly and intelligently examined the situation. The daughter thanks her mom for her guidance and agrees to reflect on it before making any decisions.

How do you think the *fundamental needs* are met in this example? Consider Direction. The mother encouraged her daughter to present her ideas so both of them would be clear on the direction the daughter felt she should take. The mother then expressed her thoughts as another option for consideration. Both had validity and shed light on the situation. What about Knowledge? The facts regarding expenses were listed so the daughter could draw her own conclusions.

What about the Essential Foundations? Was it easy to see Organization? The necessary information about the car purchase was presented in an organized fashion so the facts could speak for themselves. Purpose? The purpose of the discussion was to determine if the daughter should buy a car or not. This was clear from the beginning of the discussion, so it could

Rene Says

truly exercising their agency in a committed fashion. If you haven't earned the mantle of leader, you can't blame others for not following. However, if you have set the example and organized sufficiently, you can then correctly assess if those for whom you are responsible as a steward really do have the same vision and intentions that you do. If it is evident that people should and *can* follow but choose not to, then in the case of an employee, they've exercised their agency to leave your stewardship. If it's my child that doesn't follow, I pray!

be guided accordingly.

What about the *FaithSkills* and the *virtues* they produce? Did you notice how the mother exemplified Stewardship? (She didn't dictate how things should be done – her daughter took charge of the discussion. She also didn't interfere with her agency – she encouraged her daughter to consider the options and make her own decision.) Honesty? (She showed her daughter the checkbook with its list of car expenses so she could see that these were part of car ownership. She also gave her honest opinion when asked for it.) Influence? (Her daughter asked her mom for help with her decision, indicating that the mom had had influence in her life in the past so she trusted her judgment now.) P.S. She didn't buy any of the cars.

Our examples have indicated how a *Mothering* style of *FaithSkills* Personal Operating System can work. In both cases, the needs, foundations, skills and virtues were the same, but the processes were different. That's the beauty of the *FaithSkills* system – it is personal – you tailor it to meet your needs.

I, for one, have enjoyed enormous fulfillment through this *mothering* style Personal Operating System. One of many situations that comes to mind is a time when a company called and needed to have a big job done within a couple of days. I knew that this couldn't happen unless my team members were willing to rearrange their time off and work extra hours. I put the phone on hold and brought my team together in a huddle. We were all conditioned to doing this because of the *FaithSkills Leadership Strategies* I regularly used. I asked them how they felt about this extra work. Were they willing to do it or not? If not, I wouldn't proceed. They understood the need for an immediate decision, as they could see the red button blinking on the phone as the customer awaited our decision. My team agreed to the work. We proceeded. It was again another bonding experience for the whole team.

This was only one incident that helped us to work together to achieve the steady successes that not only brought us national and international recognition on several occasions, but also built a solid sense of family, or team, that permeated the entire business. For the most part, this was due to the constant development and application of my own *FaithSkills* Personal Operating System which in turn developed *FaithSkills* Leadership Strategies.

Permanent success and True Leadership are possible. All it takes is for you to start the process by exercising faith in yourself. If you do, your team will *assimilate your lead* and you will see that success is eminent.

It's now time that we awaken ourselves to this immense capacity that we all possess. As you recognize your spirit and the awesome physical body that you possess, you will become empowered to make the permanent positive changes you've always wanted and deserve.

Your life will be one that pivots on *when*, not *if*, you will succeed. You will know that:

You are meant to have permanent success.

You now know how to develop and apply your own *FaithSkills* Personal Operating System. Armed with the *FaithSkills* talents and virtues, you will be able to example True Leadership by *leading men with their hearts and managing their minds.*

Whether you're a mother, a father, or a grandfather, you are meant to be successful at it. Regardless of the nature of your work – a mechanic, a doctor, a flight attendant, or a business owner – it's time for you to really discover the immense power of your own personal spirit and harness it to become the permanent success that you are not only entitled to become, but expected to become.

If you do so, with a reflective mind and an open soul, you will see the success you're meant to be!

Pro-Active Reflection

CHAPTER

21

Genesis

"A New Beginning"

*O*ddly enough, the only title that came to me for this closing chapter was Genesis. No other word more clearly reflects the point at which we have arrived. It is the beginning of a different you – a new creation that has occurred through the revelatory process of reflection. You have applied this process to yourself in order to discover who you really are. You've also discovered the instruments you possess that can manifest the unlimited possibilities of what you can become – permanently!

You are now empowered to truly understand the force that drives you to succeed and how to harness it in ways you never imagined possible, *until now.* By developing your own *FaithSkills* based Personal Operating System, you will be able to exercise faith in yourself and become a beacon of positive influence at a time when the world yearns to have faith in itself.

If you doubt that *FaithSkills* work, consider this. At this very moment, you are reading my book. That action is fulfillment of my exercising faith in myself to write this book. You have also become aware of your spirit and the incredible influence it can have on your life. I hope you will incorporate it into all aspects of your life so you can become all that you want to be. You will then begin to fulfill my vision to change the way people look at themselves.

There has not been a more delicate time in the history of the world than right now. We must regain faith in ourselves, in our families and in our nations more than ever before, or we will fulfill the age-old adage: *Without faith, you are nothing.*

You are more capable of making a difference than ever before because you now know how to exercise faith in yourself. This ability will allow you to unleash the magnificent creation that you are, to the benefit of everyone who surrounds you.

One at a time, we will make the world a better place!

I am committed to this cause and want to offer continuing support to you while you develop your own personal system for achieving success. Please consider the adjoining invitation to join the Sage Academy! By doing this, you will help us create an empowering Sage Community. We have booklets, ebooks, free newsletters and success boosters to help you! Join us today and receive the benefits of these additional materials!

Remember – Keep the Faith!

P.S. Please examine the following samples of complimentary worksheets, plus much more, that you can download and print from our website. All you have to do when you visit the Sage Academy Website is to click on the charts and worksheets link at the bottom of the left navigation bar. Come and visit us at:

www.faithskills.com

Help Us Create a Sage Community
Join The Sage Academy.

"Improve Your Quality of Life Today"

Subscribe to our **No Cost** monthly e-zine called

The Message

And also

Recruit one of our Positive Providers to receive your own *Free Success Boosters* delivered twice weekly in your e-box.

We also have a special request of you -

Now that you've read the book, did you realize that you've already had a *FaithSkills* experience – either one that you've initiated yourself, or one where you've seen someone else use *FaithSkills* to "touch" the lives of others?

If so, we'd like to hear about it. We invite you to **submit your FaithSkills** experience to us by mail, email or fax, so we can share it with others and help improve their lives as *FaithSkills* have improved yours!

Along with your name and address, please include your phone number so we can contact you further if necessary. All submissions will be deemed the property of the Sage Academy and may be utilized at the sole discretion of the Sage Academy.

Visit us at: www.faithskills.com
Email us at: info@sageacademy.com
Phone us: 1–866–823–7243
Fax us: 1–604–572–6210

Or Write Us:

#9110 - 10900 NE 8th Street, 9th Flr.	15020 75th Avenue
Bellevue, Washington	Surrey, B.C.
USA 98004 - 4448	Canada V6S 6S3

APPENDIX

The following pages are samples of the daily, weekly, and monthly worksheets that have been designed by the Sage Academy to assist you in the facilitating of your *FaithSkills* assimilation process.

Designed to be user-friendly for everyone these sheets act as stimulants to nurture you in a step-by-step progression towards a life of permanent success. Because of the physical newness of *FaithSkills*, we've created these guides to enhance your spiritual familiarity of *FaithSkills* to prompt the conversion of your intelligence into the awesome *FaithSkills* talents that lay dormant within your success driven spirit.

Note: These are simply examples of the complete worksheets. Visit our website at **www.faithskills.com** to receive the complete printable worksheets.

The first series - The Daily Needs Filling Process - is intended to systematically guide you to identify your needs, by their categories, in your physical daily life. As you do, we prompt you to link them to their associated Essential Foundation. You will then gain an intimate knowledge of your *style* of operation with each and every "doorway" that you operate between your spirits' needs and its satisfying physical behavior. There is a daily set for each category to emphasize their relationship to your physical, intellectual and spiritual beings.

The Daily Needs Filling Process
Inward Needs

Day: _____

Did you recognize your spirits' inward need of	Y/N	Did you recognize how the doorway gave you access	Y/N	Record which ability, skill or talent you used today to address your need					
				Ability	Y/N	Skill	Y/N	Talent	Y/N
Acceptance		Organization		Fighter		Protective		Fearlessness	
		Order		Juggler		Justify		Cooperation	
Knowledge		Purpose		Worker		Question		Devotion	
Harmony		Balance		Follower		Respect		Obedience	
		Opposition		Builder		Administrative		Stewardship	

Day: _____

Did you recognize your spirits' inward need of	Y/N	Did you recognize how the doorway gave you access	Y/N	Record which ability, skill or talent you used today to address your need					
				Ability	Y/N	Skill	Y/N	Talent	Y/N
Acceptance		Organization		Fighter		Protective		Fearlessness	
		Order		Juggler		Justify		Cooperation	
Knowledge		Purpose		Worker		Question		Devotion	
Harmony		Balance		Follower		Respect		Obedience	
		Opposition		Builder		Administrative		Stewardship	

Day: _____

Did you recognize your spirits' inward need of	Y/N	Did you recognize how the doorway gave you access	Y/N	Record which ability, skill or talent you used today to address your need					
				Ability	Y/N	Skill	Y/N	Talent	Y/N
Acceptance		Organization		Fighter		Protective		Fearlessness	
		Order		Juggler		Justify		Cooperation	
Knowledge		Purpose		Worker		Question		Devotion	
Harmony		Balance		Follower		Respect		Obedience	
		Opposition		Builder		Administrative		Stewardship	

Notes on your Personal Daily Inward Needs Filling Process:

The Daily Needs Filling Process
Identifying Needs

Day: _____

Did you recognize your spirits' inward need of	Y/N	Did you recognize how the doorway gave you access	Y/N	Record which ability, skill or talent you used today to address your need					
				Ability	Y/N	**Skill**	Y/N	**Talent**	Y/N
Identity		Body		Player		Collaborative		Discipline	
		Spirit		Wisher		Optimistic		Humility	
		Intelligence		Tester		Analytical		Reflection	

Day: _____

Did you recognize your spirits' inward need of	Y/N	Did you recognize how the doorway gave you access	Y/N	Record which ability, skill or talent you used today to address your need					
				Ability	Y/N	**Skill**	Y/N	**Talent**	Y/N
Identity		Body		Player		Collaborative		Discipline	
		Spirit		Wisher		Optimistic		Humility	
		Intelligence		Tester		Analytical		Reflection	

Day: _____

Did you recognize your spirits' inward need of	Y/N	Did you recognize how the doorway gave you access	Y/N	Record which ability, skill or talent you used today to address your need					
				Ability	Y/N	**Skill**	Y/N	**Talent**	Y/N
Identity		Body		Player		Collaborative		Discipline	
		Spirit		Wisher		Optimistic		Humility	
		Intelligence		Tester		Analytical		Reflection	

Notes on your Personal Daily Identifying Needs Filling Process:

The Daily Needs Filling Process
Outward Needs

Day: _____

Did you recognize your spirits' inward need of	Y/N	Did you recognize how the doorway gave you access	Y/N	Record which ability, skill or talent you used today to address your need					
				Ability	Y/N	**Skill**	Y/N	**Talent**	Y/N
Direction		Laws		Complier		Attentive		Honesty	
		Agency		Chooser		Decisive		Valiance	
Empowerment		Action		Doer		Diligent		Authenticity	
Fulfillment		The Harvest		Taker		Productive		Cultivation	
		Commitment		Present		Trustworthy		Faithfulness	

Day: _____

Did you recognize your spirits' inward need of	Y/N	Did you recognize how the doorway gave you access	Y/N	Record which ability, skill or talent you used today to address your need					
				Ability	Y/N	**Skill**	Y/N	**Talent**	Y/N
Direction		Laws		Complier		Attentive		Honesty	
		Agency		Chooser		Decisive		Valiance	
Empowerment		Action		Doer		Diligent		Authenticity	
Fulfillment		The Harvest		Taker		Productive		Cultivation	
		Commitment		Present		Trustworthy		Faithfulness	

Day: _____

Did you recognize your spirits' inward need of	Y/N	Did you recognize how the doorway gave you access	Y/N	Record which ability, skill or talent you used today to address your need					
				Ability	Y/N	**Skill**	Y/N	**Talent**	Y/N
Direction		Laws		Complier		Attentive		Honesty	
		Agency		Chooser		Decisive		Valiance	
Empowerment		Action		Doer		Diligent		Authenticity	
Fulfillment		The Harvest		Taker		Productive		Cultivation	
		Commitment		Present		Trustworthy		Faithfulness	

Notes on your Personal Daily Outward Needs Filling Process:

The second sage cogitator is the Weekly Summary of your Progression to Develop *FaithSkills*.

This sheet mirrors to you the actual evolution of your transition from physical abilities (body), to intellectual skills (mind), to the ultimate, spiritual talents - *FaithSkills*.

As you will discover, with the consistent use of this form, your quality of happiness or state of being will greatly intensify as you increase your percentage of *FaithSkills* use throughout the week.

By tracking your daily use, no matter how minute, you will see that the application of *FaithSkills* definitely enhances your quality of life.

Also, **please note**; you will discover that as you master *FaithSkills,* all of your percentages will increase across the board, because you can't fully exercise a *FaithSkill* talent without manifesting or including it's relating skill and ability.

We become a well-rounded person - whole - so to speak, as we progress in the use of *FaithSkills*.

Thirdly, there is the Weekly Development of Virtues worksheet, which is intended to reveal to you the systematic process by which you are "flexing" your *FaithSkills*. It will not only demonstrate how they satisfy your fundamental needs, but will also manifest the fact that the use of *FaithSkills* will usually develop virtues, which touch others. That's because *FaithSkills* are most effectively developed in acts of service. It's where they're the most potent, and thus, the most energizing.

Weekly Summary of Your Progression to Develop FaithSkills

BODY	M	T	W	T	F	S	S
Present							
Taker							
Doer							
Chooser							
Complier							
Player							
Wisher							
Tester							
Fighter							
Juggler							
Worker							
Follower							
Builder							
Daily Total							

Weekly Total _____ ÷ 91 = _____ %

MIND	M	T	W	T	F	S	S
Trustworthy							
Productive							
Diligent							
Decisive							
Attentive							
Collaborative							
Optimistic							
Analytical							
Protective							
Justify							
Question							
Respect							
Administrative							
Daily Total							

Weekly Total _____ ÷ 91 = _____ %

SPIRIT	M	T	W	T	F	S	S
Faithfulness							
Cultivation							
Authenticity							
Valiance							
Honesty							
Discipline							
Humility							
Reflection							
Fearlessness							
Cooperation							
Devotion							
Obedience							
Stewardship							
Daily Total							

Weekly Total _____ ÷ 91 = _____ %

293

Weekly Development of Virtues

Did you "Flex" your FaithSkill of	M	T	W	T	F	S	S	Did you satisfy your need for	M	T	W	T	F	S	S	Did you develop the virtue of	M	T	W	T	F	S	S
Faithfulness								FULFILLMENT								CHARITY							
Cultivation																							
Authenticity								EMPOWERMENT								HONOR							
Valiance																							
Honesty								DIRECTION								INFLUENCE							
Discipline																							
Humility								IDENTITY								INTEGRITY							
Reflection																							
Fearlessness								HARMONY								PATIENCE							
Cooperation																							
Devotion								KNOWLEDGE								SELF-RELIANCE							
Obedience								ACCEPTANCE								DISCERNMENT							
Stewardship																							

With *FaithSkills* Everyday is a Success is designed to ensure your development into a permanent positive thinker. By manifesting to you how the use of *FaithSkills* directs your every action to contribute to your spirits fundamental needs satisfaction, you become empowered by every thought and action you create in this life.

You will witness how your identifying, addressing, and satisfying of your fundamental needs improves not only your world but that of those who are in contact with you.

Monitor it daily, weekly and monthly by carrying forward your increasing percentage on each weekly sheet.

Our life here, in this physical existence, is meant to be one of constant progression which in itself requires change, which in turn, translates into success. But only if we're cognizant of it and thus chart it's never-ending occurrences.

We are meant to be a permanent success and this life is the opportunity we have to manifest it.

Use this worksheet to awaken your physical and intellectual beings to become whole and confirm what your spirit knows is meant to happen!

Be the permanent success you are meant to be!

With *FaithSkills* Everyday is a Success	M	T	W	T	F	S	S
Did you identify one or more of your spirit's fundamental needs?							
Did you address one or more of your spirit's fundamental needs?							
Did you satisfy one or more of your spirit's fundamental needs with a *FaithSkill?*							
Did you improve someone else's world with the use of your FaithSkills?							
Did you touch and improve someone's life with a virtue you developed with the use of FaithSkills?							

Your Daily Total: Monday   _____ ÷ 5 = _____ %
Tuesday   _____ ÷ 5 = _____ %
Wednesday   _____ ÷ 5 = _____ %
Thursday   _____ ÷ 5 = _____ %
Friday   _____ ÷ 5 = _____ %
Saturday   _____ ÷ 5 = _____ %
Sunday   _____ ÷ 5 = _____ %
Weekly Total: _____ ÷ 35 = _____ %

Monthly Progression: 1st Week _____   4th Week _____
2nd Week _____   5th Week _____
3rd Week _____

296

Rules and Conduct of a Sage

- Know that you will improve the world
- Contribute to the mission daily
- Always think of the greater good
- Listen more than you speak
- Always listen with your spirit first
- Confidence, not pride
- All ideas are good - share them
- Earn and give full trust, nothing less
- Work hard, work quickly, work whenever
- Know when to work alone and when to work together
- Invent different ways of working
- The customer defines the quality
- Know that together we can do anything
- Reflect

Remember: "Keep the Faith!"

courtesy of the Sage Academy

The Sage Academy

OUR MISSION STATEMENT

Guiding Individuals to Discover
their Innate Nature to Succeed; by
Awakening the Power of Reflection
in their Daily Lives, Thereby,
Empowering them to Achieve
Unrealized Levels of Success
Through *FaithSkills*.

OUR VISION

To change the way people
look at themselves.

INDEX

Order Form

Give the Gift of *Permanent Success* to your Friends, Family, Team Members and Colleagues!

Check your leading Bookstore or Order Here

YES, I want _____ copies of *FaithSkills – Discover Permanent Success* at $19.95 each, plus $4.95 shipping per book. All applicable taxes will be added. All prices are in U.S. funds.

YES, I would like to take advantage of your offer for a bulk discount order for the benefit of my firm, association, or family members. Available on fax or phone orders only. Please call for details.

Please Charge My:

___Visa ___MasterCard ___Amex ___Discover

Name:_____

Organization:_____

Address:_____

City/State/Province:_____

Zip/Postal:_____Phone:_____

Card#_____Exp Date:_____

# of Books:_____ Signature_____

How Did You Hear About This Book?_____

_____

Call this number if you wish to place a Credit Card order:
1–866–823–7243
Fax Orders: 1–604–572–6210 Email:info@sageacademy.com

The Book That Others Call
"The Manual to Success"!

Whether you're a Parent, Business Owner, Entrepreneur, or simply the one who's responsible for the results of the day, you'll gain Tenfold from this Book. You'll discover how to build your own life of permanent successes and be empowered to positively influence many people in ways you couldn't perceive possible – until now. As you build upon these profound, proven foundations of success, you will also be able to maintain sustained levels of satisfaction for yourself and those for whom you are responsible – like never before.

Come and Discover:

- What that "Force" is within you that yearns for success and satisfy it forever.
- "Who you really are" and how that awareness can positively affect the image of your family and business in ways you never dreamed of.
- How to get off the "success treadmill" and produce the sustained levels of satisfaction you deserve and need.
- The "reference points" for permanent success and the never changing map that can lead you to create the permanent positive changes you've always wanted.
- How to literally exercise "faith in yourself" and unleash the enormous powers that you possess to immediately change the way you look at yourself and the circumstances in which you live.
- A heightened level of deep "inner confidence" from a new clear vision of your true purpose in life – it will lead and influence your family, business and friends to new levels of total fulfillment.
- True leadership by inspiring others to example the powerful "code of conduct" that you carefully create and diligently follow to rapidly move forward in your own personal success building strategy.

Read This Book and
Change the Way You Look at Life -

Forever!